MATT BUSBY'S
MANCHESTER UNITED
SCRAPBOOK

IF . . .

ONE of the smallest—yet most important—words in the English language is . . . IF. And now and again I find myself thinking: 'What if . . .?' Indeed, there are times when I permit myself a smile and imagine that, had I made a different decision on one important occasion, it might have been Matt Busby of Liverpool, and not of Manchester United.

The thought tempts me to speculate that if this HAD happened, Bill Shankly might even have wound up at Old Trafford, instead of Anfield!

Then again, I might have started out in my working life as a miner and finished up still a pitman . . . or I might now have made a bit of a name for myself as a pioneer of Soccer in the United States. The reality of it all, however, is that October 22, 1980, marked the 35th anniversary of my arrival at Manchester United. And the dawn of a new decade was marked by my appointment as president, after service as manager and as a director. Needless to say, thereby hangs a tale.

And thereby hangs a tale

Matt Busby

MATT BUSBY'S MANCHESTER UNITED SCRAPBOOK

by
Sir Matt Busby, Kt., C.B.E.

**PICTORIAL
PRESENTATIONS**

SOUVENIR PRESS

Sir Matt Busby would like to express his thanks to STAN LIVERSEDGE for
his collaboration in the compiling of this book and to acknowledge the
following for the use of pictures:
Press Association, Peter Beckett, Cheshire Press Studios (Bramhall), County
Press (Wigan), Daily Express, the Football Association, J. Hampson
(Didsbury), Jim Harvey, Lawrence of Stretford, Liverpool F.C., Daily Mail,
Daily Mirror, Manchester Evening News, Harry Ormesher, Sunday People,
United Press International, The Weekly News, A. Wilkes (West Bromwich).

First published 1980 by Souvenir Press Ltd,
43 Great Russell Street, London WC1B 3PA
and simultaneously in Canada

ISBN 0 285 62469 5 casebound
ISBN 0 285 62456 3 paperback

Filmset and printed in Great Britain by
BAS Printers Limited, Over Wallop, Hampshire

CONTENTS

IN THE BEGINNING

THIS was what Matt Busby inherited when he took up the challenge of becoming manager of Manchester United. The Old Trafford ground had been damaged during the blitz, and some years were to pass before it became recognisable as a football stadium again. Players were still in the Forces or just returning from the war, and it was a time of austerity all round. But Matt Busby had some things going for him . . . he was a track-suit manager, fit and enthusiastic, and he had his own ideas about building a team.

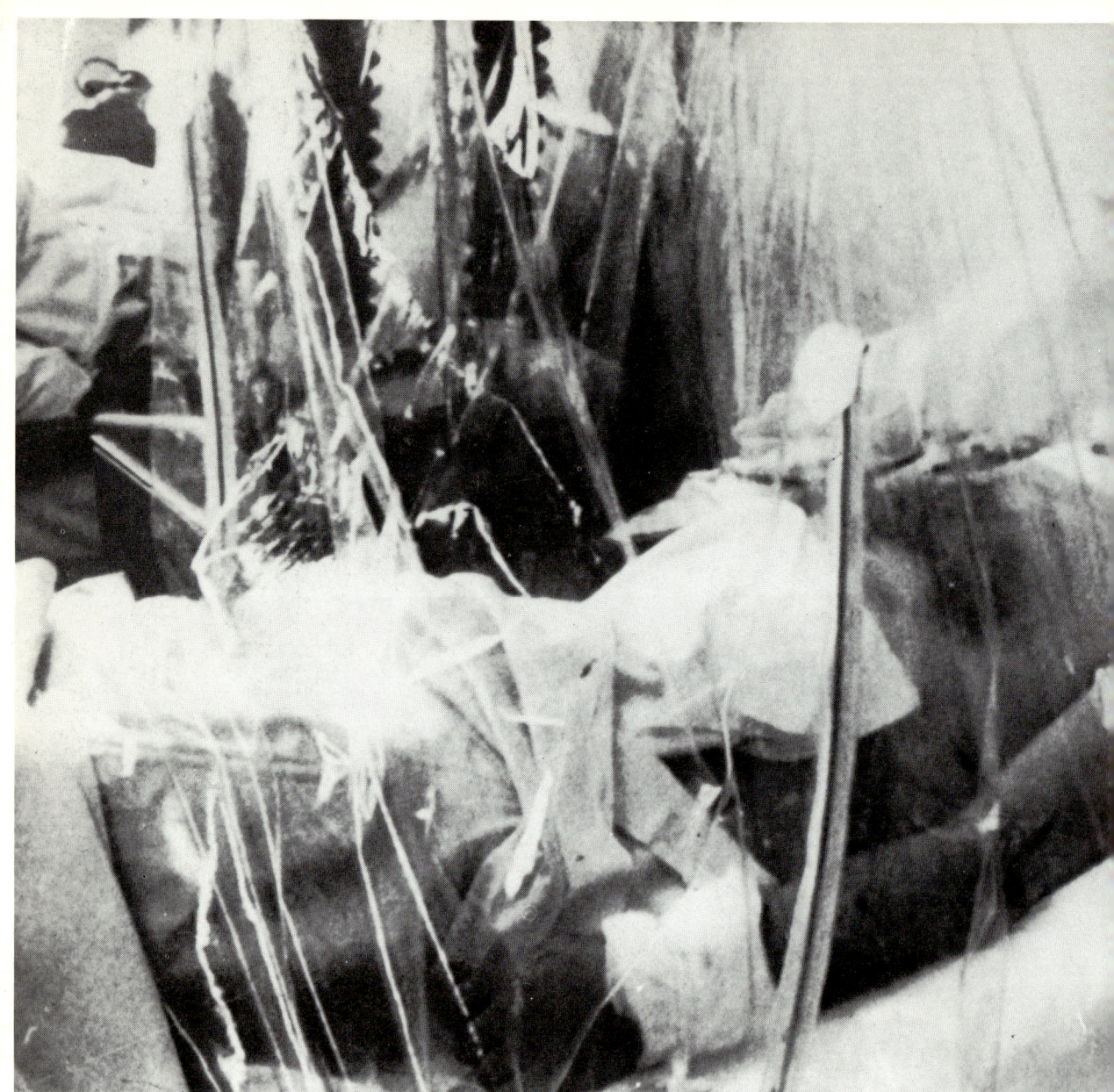

1958

TWO PICTURES which show, in stark contrast, the twists and turns Matt Busby's career took during his years as manager of Manchester United. Above, after the air crash at Munich in February, 1958, a picture that shocked the world, as he hovered between life and death while lying in a hospital bed at the Rechts der Isar hospital. His injuries were so severe that survival was a word only to be whispered, rather than proclaimed with confidence. But survive Matt Busby did . . . to make Manchester United all-conquering in Europe. And the proof is there 10 years on, as he holds aloft the glittering European Cup.

A matter of life and death

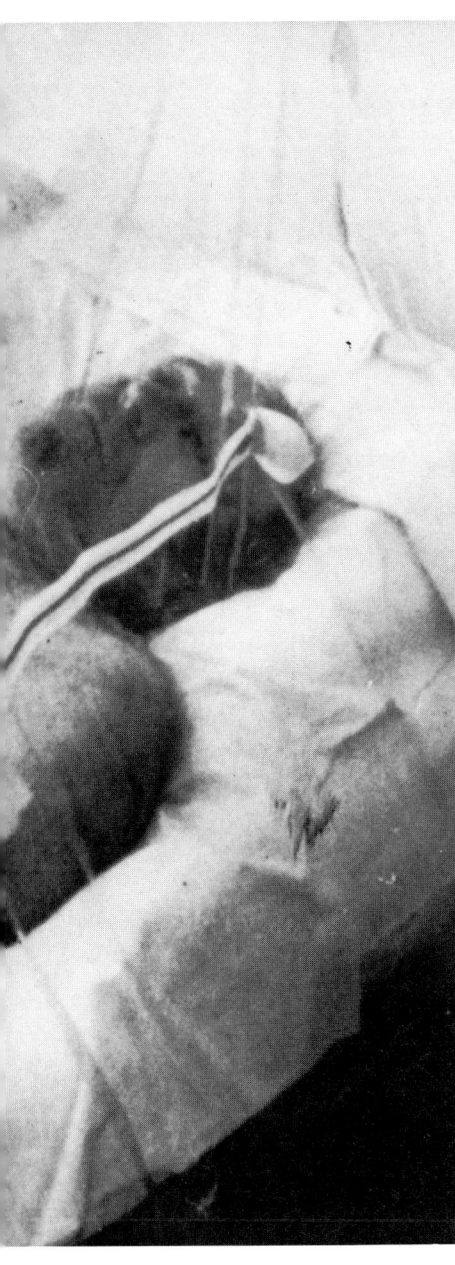

1968

At last—the
European Cup

1980

AS Sir Matt Busby surveys Old Trafford today, 35 years after he arrived as Manchester United's manager, he can see the fruits of his labours. A magnificent stadium rises skywards, and the team regularly plays in front of crowds topping the 50,000 mark.

TWO views of the famous Stretford End—top right and towards the left of the picture, where the massed ranks of the United fans stand and cheer their team. And right, an unusual, bird's-eye view of the Stretford End, as pigeons take possession—if only temporarily—of the goalmouth.

SO WE NEVER DID GO TO AMERICA . . .

THE Lanarkshire village of Orbiston had one doctor, and his name was Douglas. I was born in a two-roomed pitman's cottage in Orbiston, and within minutes of my arrival, Dr. Douglas was telling my mother: 'A footballer has come into this house today.'

It may have been a flight of fancy, or pure guesswork; but the forecast turned out to be accurate—although there were one or two diversions along the way. Despite my constant preoccupation with kicking a ball around, my headmaster thought I might make a teacher, and he suggested to my widowed mother (a sniper's bullet had killed my father during the first world war) that I should stay at school until I was 18.

However, my mother was of a mind to emigrate to the United States, and adamant that if the family sought a new life there, I would not be left in Scotland. She was obdurate about another thing: that I would not spend my working life down the pit . . . but a miner I became, as the family waited for the visa that would transport us to a new world across the Atlantic.

Meanwhile, when I wasn't down the pit I was playing football, and I graduated from one local side to another, moving up the scale each time, until the day came when Manchester City offered me a career in the game. So we never did go to America—not to live, at any rate; although I have visited the States several times on football business, and I was able to send my mother there for a holiday so that she could renew acquaintance with other members of the family.

February 1928 was the month of destiny for me. I arrived in Manchester to become a City player for the princely wage of £5 a week (£4 during the close season). I played for City in every forward position, and failed to impress; and at one stage I had packed my bags and was ready to go back home. 'I feel I am out of my sphere in football,' was what I wrote to the girl who was to become my wife.

By the autumn of 1930 I wasn't even a regular in City's reserve team—then came the turning point, when I was tried for the first time at right-half. Something clicked, and my career began to blossom.

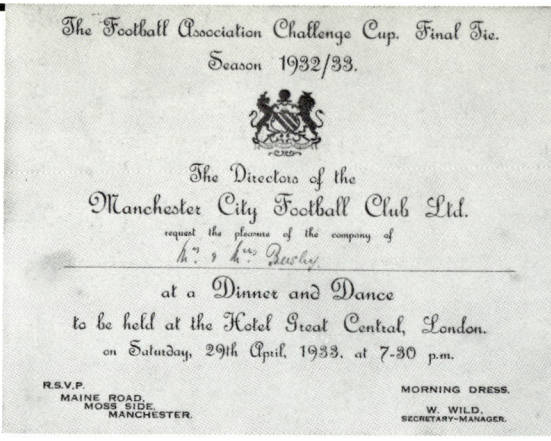

ALMOST 50 years ago . . . and Matt Busby was making his acquaintance with Wembley then, as a member of Manchester City's F.A. Cup-final teams in 1933 and 1934. The invitation cards (the one below is autographed by City players) are for the 1933 final banquet.

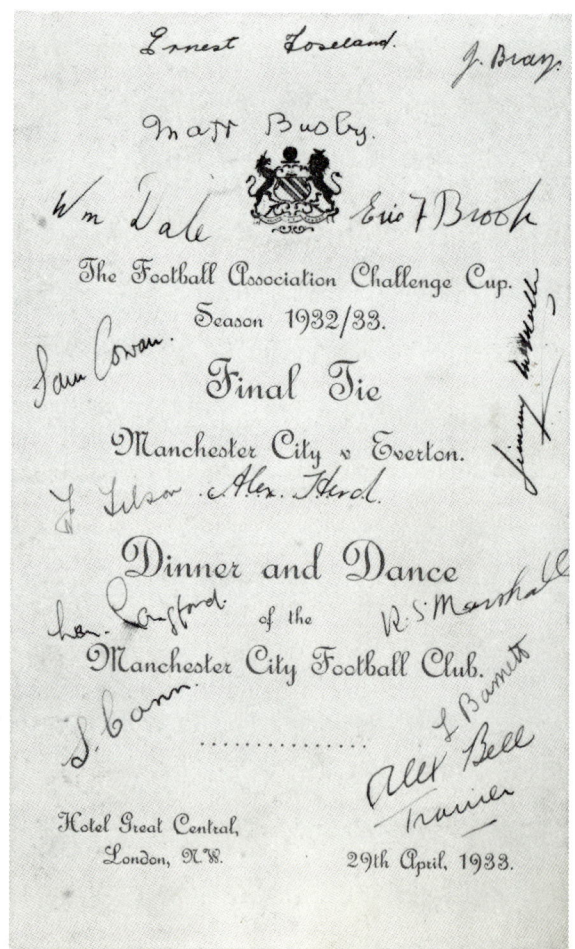

MANCHESTER BLUES . .

MATT BUSBY recalls his days at Manchester City. Far left, Sam Cowan, who skippered the Blues in the 1933 and 1934 F.A. Cup finals; left: listening to the Cup draw; below: action in the 1934 final, as City attack the Portsmouth goal. Then come the men who won the Cup for City in 1934, with shots below also of training spins and relaxation at Southport baths.

From the third team to the reserves to the First Division side . . . promotion was swift, success was sweet. And one City director said it all when he told me: 'I'm glad to see you making a good shape at wing-half, because as a forward you were a washout.'

City in those days were THE club in Manchester. United were the poor relations. And I must admit that I never nurtured any secret ambition to switch my allegiance from the blue jersey to the red. But it happened . . . when I joined Liverpool.

Before that, I had tasted success when City went to the F.A. Cup final in 1933 and 1934. We lost against Everton and won against Portsmouth. The final against Everton taught me one thing which stuck in my mind years later, when Manchester United went to Wembley—get there in time, but not so soon that there is nothing to do but allow nerves to take over.

The reasons for my deciding on a transfer from City were varied, but I ended my career at Maine-road an unhappy man. I had been out of action for almost a year because of a leg injury; my wife, Jean, was constantly under the doctor around that time; and at the club itself, there were irritations which made me feel the time had come to make a move. When City agreed to release me, Liverpool just happened to be the club which produced an offer to suit my employers, and so I landed on Merseyside—where Everton then were the top dogs, as Liverpool struggled to avoid relegation.

Players were growing old together, and manager George Kay taught me another lesson: that a team boss must be a fighter, just like his team. And I learned something from Liverpool about man-management when they kept a player on top wages even when he wasn't getting a game, and when they rewarded his loyal service with a second benefit.

When the war came, I embarked on a new career, as a soldier, and if at first I felt a misfit, by the end of my service I had graduated to company sergeant-major. But I had lost six years of my Soccer career, and with a wife and two bairns to feed, I knew that, at 35, I must look for a future off the playing field.

I had been to Wembley, I had played for Scotland at Hampden Park; but memories wouldn't pay the grocery bills, and on my demob in 1945 I faced up to the facts. Luck smiled on me then, for I received more than one offer to stay in football, on the backroom side.

Reading's manager then was Joe Edelston, and he asked me if I fancied becoming his right-hand man.

There was also an offer for me to become the manager of Ayr United. But the major offer was one from the club for which I had been playing . . . Liverpool.

Liverpool came up with a five-year contract and a job as coach. Verbally, I agreed to take the job, but at a meeting with the board—and before I had put pen to paper—I made it crystal clear that my aim was to break into management. I wanted to be my own boss and put my ideas to the test.

The directors told me they hoped I would be able to take some of the weight off George Kay, but still I hesitated. Had I signed that contract, who knows what would have happened? As it turned out, George fell ill and had to quit. But before I had arrived at my decision, someone else had made one. It changed the course of my life.

A gentleman called Mr. J. W. Gibson wanted to see me, and he was the chairman of hard-up, bombed-out Manchester United. He had taken charge and was determined to clear the debts, and I was the man he wanted as manager.

Not surprisingly, the Liverpool directors were somewhat displeased when I told them that I must decline their offer because I had decided to become the manager of United. There seemed to be a misunderstanding, too, because for some reason they had the impression that I was going to Old Trafford as player-manager.

There was even talk about demanding a transfer fee from United, and my relations with the Liverpool board became a little strained. Indeed, it was a case of parting 'brass rags', for after I had accepted an invitation from George Kay to make my farewell appearance at Anfield in an exhibition game, he phoned me back. The message was this: 'There's been a change of mind here. The directors don't want you to play.'

So I didn't make that sentimental journey back to Anfield, where I had spent the nine happiest years of my footballing life . . . but I am delighted to add that, as time went by, I was welcomed back by Liverpool on many occasions, and for years I have considered their directors and officials among my great friends in football.

More than that: I was a player there when Bob Paisley arrived as a youngster, and it has given me pleasure to see him succeed as a manager, for I know from my own experiences in the 'hot seat' that it is not easy to make that transition, even if you have learned a great deal along the way.

LIVERPOOL days . . . and above, two of Matt Busby's Anfield team-mates, Tommy Bradshaw and Jimmy McDougall. Right: Matt Busby leads out Liverpool for a derby game against Everton. And immediately below, he wears an unhappy expression as Leeds stick the ball in Liverpool's net.

15

BLITZED BY BOMBS, AND HEAD OVER HEELS IN DEBT

ANYONE who imagines that I had no doubts when I signed on at Manchester United on October 22, 1945, can think again. This was a First Division club—but, to be frank, in name only. The ground had been blitzed, the club was head over heels in debt—something my chairman was determined to eradicate—and I had to prove that I was big enough for a job of mammoth proportions.

There is a question which I would sometimes like to put to the thousands of fans who on Saturdays make their pilgrimage to Old Trafford now—many of whom had not been born by the time football swung into gear again after the war. 'Would you believe,' I would ask, 'seeing Old Trafford as it is now, that in 1945 the dressing-rooms were derelict, there were no offices for staff, and no training facilities?'

I had two things going for me: I was fit, and I had plenty of ideas. I put one of my ideas into practice straight away. Some managers were seldom seen on the training pitch, but I used my fitness as an asset and mucked in with my players. I was a track-suit manager, young enough and fit enough to go through the hard graft with them.

The club offices were at the Cornbrook Cold Stores—Mr. Gibson's own business premises—and we relied upon the generosity of Manchester City to play home matches at Maine-road. Furthermore, United were in the red to the tune of £15,000 . . . and, believe me, 35 years ago that was a lot of money.

I knew there were half a dozen really good players, and that the team had possibilities. But there was such a long way to go before Manchester United could claim to be top of the pile. We played in the League North, immediately after the war, and our first game was against Bolton Wanderers.

This was the first team I ever chose, as manager of United: Crompton; Walton, Roach; Warner, Whalley, Cockburn; Worrall, Carey, Smith, Rowley, Wrigglesworth. We were 16th in the table, and Johnny Carey was playing his first match for two years.

LEFT to right, reading along the top row: Mr. J. W. Gibson, the man who persuaded Matt Busby to become United's manager; Johnny Carey, who led the team on the field; and Jimmy Delaney, who turned out to be a bargain buy.

ABOVE (left to right): Jack Rowley, Stan Pearson, Henry Cockburn, and below, Charlie Mitten, Allenby Chilton and John Anderson, who wound up with a winner's medal after being a last-minute choice for United's 1948 F.A. Cup-final side.

There were other players on the staff—Stan Pearson, Allenby Chilton, Johnny Morris, Charlie Mitten—but not all of them had been demobbed, and some on the club's books were coming to the close of their playing careers.

Decisions are sometimes difficult, but they have to be made, and when I had taken stock, I knew that some players had to be replaced. I made positional switches, I tried new ideas in training, I did anything which I thought would improve the side.

By the end of the season we had climbed to fourth place, and I had embarked upon a policy of finding

A ROUND of golf for relaxation . . . and Matt Busby makes a point to Tommy McNulty, Stan Pearson and Johnny Downie.

young talent to replace the old heads. There had been no reserve-team football during the war, so the assembly line of talent had broken down. It was a case of going out and finding new faces and making footballers from unknowns.

I felt that the team I had at the end of the season was considerably better than the one with which we had started, and that is no disrespect to any of the players who had worn United's colours during that term. By the end of the season, Chilton, Rowley, Pearson, Johnny Aston and Jimmy Delaney had broken through to the side—although in Jimmy's case, it was hardly a case of 'breaking through', for he was a vastly experienced player.

Some you win, some you lose . . . and there are times when you must be prepared to gamble. Carey and Aston, for instance, both began as forwards and developed into the finest full-back pairing in the country; Chilton was converted from wing-half to centre-half; and all three went on to play for their respective countries.

And Delaney? Here was one of those gambles which paid off, for this Scottish international had been out of football for about a year with a shoulder injury when I signed him. Indeed, people warned me off him—'He's brittle-boned,' they said—but I felt that at £4,000, Jimmy would be a worthwhile risk as a short-term investment.

He gave Manchester United six magnificent seasons, and when he finally picked up his boots and left Old Trafford—with my heartfelt thanks, I might add—we recouped £3,500 of the £4,000 we had paid for him. And he gave Aberdeen and several other clubs top-class service before he called it a day.

I should mention here, also, that Stan Pearson turned out to be a winner, for this quiet, unassuming footballer showed that he could be the brains of the attack, and that he was dependable week in, week out. Nothing flashy—but he could size up a situation in the blink of an eyelid, and he really could make the forward line tick.

Pearson was in good company, of course, with Morris, Rowley, Mitten and Delaney alongside him, but he was gifted more than most with the ability to score goals inside the box: not just goals, but what I call clever goals . . . he could glide and flick the ball with his head as few players have been able to do.

Rowley was a different proposition—the 'Gunner' could hammer shots goalward with the ferocity of a howitzer blasting off, and it didn't seem to matter whether the pass had come to him on his right foot or his left. He could adapt equally effectively, in any one of four forward positions (the right wing was the exception).

More than one well-meaning person marked my card that Jack Rowley could be difficult to handle, but never did he give me less than 100 per cent., and he certainly never struck me as a member of the 'awkward brigade'.

Morris was the 'cheeky' type of player who, when the mood took him, could demoralise defences as he darted here and there and, on occasion, had the temerity to 'nutmeg' even the opposing goalkeeper. It was a sad day for me when he and I found that we had to agree to differ, and so he moved on to Derby County.

Mitten and I had a difference of opinion, too, for there came a time when the lure of what seemed like El Dorado proved too strong for Charlie, and he joined the ill-fated trek by a few English stars to Bogota, in Colombia. When I heard that a Bogota representative was offering big money to stars prepared to venture to South America, I called my players together and warned them that they faced trouble from club, League and F.A. And I added: 'You may find Bogota isn't the Soccer mecca you imagine.'

However, Charlie was bitten by the bug. I learned about it when we were on tour in America and enjoying a drink in the Astor Club in New York. He came over and told me: 'I've been offered a signing fee of £2,500, plus £50 a week, plus bonuses . . . it's an offer I can't refuse.'

When I realised I couldn't dissuade him, I told

17

ALL THE sweet taste of success is summed up in these pictures of United players, wives and fans. The war has been and gone, and Manchester United have begun to carve their name with pride in Soccer's roll of honour.

THE DAYS when rival fans could mingle together in safety—even at an F.A. Cup semi-final. It's Manchester United versus Derby County at Sheffield in March, 1948 . . . and United are on their way to Wembley, and a victory there over Blackpool.

Charlie that if—as I felt would happen—he ever returned to England, there would be no place for him at Manchester United. Charlie went—and, to his credit, he honoured his contract with Bogota. When he returned, he was looking for a job, but though United could still have done with his footballing skill, I stuck to my word, and he was transferred to Fulham for a good-sized fee.

Players such as I have mentioned—and I've saved others until later—formed the nucleus of a team which, I felt, could take Manchester United to honours within a few seasons of the rebuilding job I had undertaken at Old Trafford. I was not disappointed, either.

In season 1946–47 United claimed the runners-up place in the First Division, and people were beginning to talk about a side which played football with the kind of flair and style which I had hoped to develop.

Indeed, we were going forward faster than I could have dreamed of, and it wasn't only in terms of getting results. The supporters were rolling up in ever-increasing numbers, and even the bank manager was beginning to smile, for in the two seasons from 1945 to 1947, Manchester United were able to report that there had been a profit of close on £60,000.

Ironically, perhaps, when we finished second it had to be to my old club, Liverpool . . . but that wasn't bad, all things considered, although I must admit that even after two seasons and some success, I still felt I could make improvements.

'BACK UNITED FOR THE CUP!'

I think I can claim that, as a manager, I wasn't given to shouting the odds, but at the start of season 1947–48 I felt so sure that Manchester United were poised for the breakthrough that I stuck out my neck and said: 'My lads are going to win the F.A. Cup . . . don't back anyone else.'

That advice was given privately, to a friend—and his answer was this: 'Don't kid yourself, Matt. I've seen the League table, and there are 15 teams better than United, if that's any guide.' Yes, we were lying in 16th place when I offered my piece of advice . . . and my friend decided to take it, despite his reservations. He invested a few pounds in United, and got odds of 25 to one. At the end of the season, he picked up quite a packet, when United had won the Cup.

Deep down, I knew that we had not been having luck when it came to scoring goals; if we could change this, I believed we could win something, and the Cup seemed the best bet. When our luck turned, it did so with a vengeance, as we went to Molineux and whipped Wolves 6–2. However, we couldn't overtake Arsenal for the league title and finished the season as runners-up again . . .

We had a scare or two in the Cup, but it all came right in the end. Our first tie was at Villa Park, and the opposition scored almost from the kick-off; but we gave Villa a footballing lesson, going in at half-time 5–1 ahead. The second half produced a tremendous battle, though, as Villa made it 5–2, 5–3, then 5–4, and there were signs of panic in United's ranks. But Stan Pearson chipped in with a late goal which knocked the heart out of Villa.

That proved our toughest confrontation on the road to Wembley—even Derby County in the semi-final didn't give us as much trouble. Derby scored all right, but a Pearson hat-trick despatched them, and left us with the job of beating Blackpool at Wembley.

I worried more about players being injured during the six-week gap between semi-final and final than I did about United beating Blackpool, even though they had Stanley Matthews and Stan Mortensen, Harry Johnston and Eddie Shimwell among a galaxy of star players.

When I came to pick my team, I took a gamble by leaving out the experienced Jack Warner and pitching in a reserve, Johnny Anderson, while Blackpool sprang a surprise by omitting Jimmy McIntosh, who had played in every round, and playing Alec Munro. My decision was made because I felt that Anderson could give us added strength at right-half, and it came off. When it was all over, Johnny said to me: 'I always thought I'd give my life for a Cup-winner's medal . . . now it's happened so suddenly, I just can't believe it.'

Manchester United have been involved in more than one controversial Cup final since the war, and the 1948 final produced a penalty early on which was bitterly disputed by my players, for when Mortensen was downed by Chilton, the referee awarded a spot-kick . . . yet photographs later clearly showed Morty to have been in the 'D' outside the 18-yard box when he fell.

When Shimwell scored from the spot, it didn't shake my conviction that United would finish as winners, and Jack Rowley's equaliser only hardened my belief in victory. But when Morty—then the most dangerous striker in the world, in my view—scored for Blackpool, it meant that we were trailing again as half-time came round.

It was skipper Johnny Carey who, during the ten-minute break, provided the necessary inspiration for his team-mates. He urged them: 'Keep on playing football as you have been doing . . . the goals are bound to come.' His utter confidence stoked up the rest of the team, and we drew level for the second time by scoring one of the 'brainiest' goals I have ever seen.

United won a free-kick near the touchline, and before anyone realised it, Johnny Morris had placed the ball and whipped it into Blackpool's penalty area, where Jack Rowley stood unmarked. His header was in the net before Blackpool knew what had hit them.

From then on, United were the bosses: Stan Pearson made it 3–2, and Johnny Anderson, the player on whom I had gambled, tucked away another scoring chance so that United ran out 4–2 winners.

That final was declared by many of the 100,000 who saw it at Wembley to be the finest ever played,

and Blackpool deserved credit as much as United for making it such a feast of football. As King George VI said to Carey, when he presented the Cup, 'I have thoroughly enjoyed the game.'

The King might have had a shock had he known what Carey had been urged to say to him! For in a letter to Johnny before the final, a fellow Irishman had suggested that United's captain should 'ask the King what he thinks about partition when you meet him.'

This was the team which did United proud that day: Crompton; Carey, Aston; Anderson, Chilton, Cockburn; Delaney, Morris, Rowley, Pearson, Mitten.

Jack Crompton has been at Old Trafford a long time now, and has given the club great service. Johnny Aston, who also served on the backroom side for a spell, was so loyal to United that he was willing to prejudice his chance of England honours by volunteering to play anywhere in his club's side, when we had injury problems.

As for Chilton, he had come through a hard time, for in his early days at United he had to endure severe criticism. It seemed that whenever he made a mistake

UNITED'S Squad of players when they won the F.A. Cup in 1948. Back row (left to right): Manager Matt Busby, Johnny Anderson, Jack Warner, Allenby Chilton, Jack Crompton, Henry Cockburn, John Aston, Tom Curry (trainer). Front row: Jimmy Delaney, Johnny Morris, Johnny Carey, Jack Rowley, Stan Pearson, Charlie Mitten.

WE'VE won the Cup! United skipper Johnny Carey gets a hand up from team-mates Charlie Mitten and Jack Crompton, after the 1948 final against Blackpool.

a goal resulted against us, and he was often made a scapegoat by people for what, in my view, was pure bad luck.

I continued to back him, and he proved me right. He also proved a tower of strength when I introduced youngsters into the team, for he nursed them along and his confidence brushed off on to them.

I have mentioned Johnny Carey before, but I must recall the rather dramatic circumstances of how United came to sign him. The club's chief scout at the time, Louis Rocca, had gone to Dublin to watch another player. Instead, he came back with a recommendation that Carey should be signed.

The Irishman's arrival in Manchester was unheralded. Indeed, when Johnny saw a newspaper bill proclaiming 'United's Big Capture' he felt surprised to be so flattered . . . until he read that the club had signed centre-forward Ernie Thompson from Blackburn Rovers for £5,000. At the foot of the story he read: 'United have also signed a junior from Ireland. His name is J. Carey.'

In the end Thompson did not play more than a score of first-team games for United. Carey stayed to play hundreds, as he became one of the great footballers of all time. He was at Old Trafford when I arrived, and I quickly made him club captain. That was how much I thought of his wisdom and ability.

As a player, he was an artist, and even today one example of his skill remains vivid in my memory. During a game, an opposing player lofted the ball— and it was a precision pass—over Carey's head to the

left-winger. It was too high for Carey to nod away, perfectly placed for the winger to gain possession and leave the right-back stranded.

But, just as Carey appeared beaten, he swung around until he had his back to the man who had passed the ball; then he caught it on his instep, juggled it for a couple of seconds on his foot, flipped the ball over his head, turned around . . . and placed a perfect pass to one of his own team-mates. It was a touch of Soccer genius which won ungrudging applause from fans of both teams.

Carey, quiet and deep thinking, also had a sense of shrewd humour, as he demonstrated when we were on tour in America. Our sight-seeing coach stopped close by a big New York store. The name above the store suggested that one partner was Irish, the other Jewish. Johnny pointed to the sign and said: 'I'll bet I know which of those two does all the hard work . . .'

He, and players like Delaney, Cockburn, Pearson, Morris, Rowley and Mitten, helped to put not only Manchester United but Matt Busby on the Soccer map, and that is something I have never forgotten. But, of course, no matter how much a manager may admire his team, he has to be a realist, and this means recognition of the fact that even great footballers cannot combat the years for ever.

My over-riding responsibility was to the club, and so I had to think hard and long about how we could plan for the future. That meant thinking in terms of breaking up a truly fine side . . . and it was something which, as time went by, had to be done.

'I'LL MAKE—OR BREAK—UNITED!'

IF 1948 was notable because of United's F.A. Cup-final triumph, it was also the year which brought me another managerial job—taking charge of the Great Britain Olympic Soccer team. And you can take it from me that trying to produce a winning team from more than two dozen part-time footballers from four countries calls for some managerial expertise!

Most of the players were strangers to each other, and all except one—Bob Hardisty, the Bishop Auckland star who had played alongside me at Middlesbrough during the war—had never met Matt Busby. So in that respect we started level. And fortunately for me, the staff at Old Trafford gave invaluable help. Men like Carey, Rowley and Pearson taught my new team how to improve their play, and the backroom staff weighed in with help and advice.

I handled the Olympic hopefuls as I handled my professionals: I worked them like slaves, treated them like men—and they responded without a word of complaint. They beat Holland 4–3 at Highbury, defeated France 1–0 at Craven Cottage, and came unstuck only in the semi-finals when, at Highbury, they lost 3–1 to a Yugoslav side which was virtually all professionals (a similar team from Yugoslavia later drew with the full England eleven at Highbury).

But while I enjoyed my excursion into the realm of the Olympics, all the time at the back of my mind was the knowledge that at club level, I faced another problem . . . how to maintain the success we had achieved, and when to start ringing the changes.

Manchester United finished as First Division runners-up in 1947, 1948 and 1949, were unplaced in 1950, claimed second place again in 1951 and crowned it all by claiming the championship at the end of the season 1951–52, finishing with 57 points—four ahead of second-placed Tottenham Hotspur.

If there was a feeling of euphoria among our supporters at that time, I did not share it, and at the 1952 annual general meeting of Manchester United I spelled out my view: that it would be rash to be optimistic—unless drastic changes were made. For I recognised that a great team was growing old.

I didn't relish the task of breaking up the side, of replacing players who had rendered such distinguished and loyal service; but it had to be done. And I told United's shareholders the blunt facts . . . promising that behind the names which had won such acclaim were unknowns worth hundreds of

UNITED'S players celebrate, after winning the League championship in season 1951–52. Left to right: Henry Cockburn, John Aston, Johnny Berry, Tommy McNulty, Roger Byrne, Reg. Allen and Johnny Carey, as assistant trainer Bill Inglis dispenses the champagne.

thousands of pounds, youngsters on the staff who were poised to take over.

I knew people thought I was trying a con trick, that I was bluffing and, perhaps, only preparing them in advance for disappointment: for I also said that the youngsters, while talented, would need time to blend and achieve similar success. But I meant what I said, and events proved my claims justified.

Behind the scenes, we had been nursing players like Duncan Edwards, Eddie Colman, David Pegg, Jackie Blanchflower, and I knew, also, that if I waited too long to give them their chance, they could become dissatisfied and be asking to get away.

Season 1952–53 began with United fielding the side which had captured the championship, but I was in a restless mood because I knew we were not producing the football of old. Matters came to a head after we had beaten Aston Villa 1–0 at Old Trafford, for the game itself had been terrible to watch.

At a board meeting, I told the directors: 'The time for action has come. It's got to be drastic, and I'm going to make sweeping changes. Even if everyone says I'm crazy, I'm going to make the move which will make or break Manchester United.' And I made that move in a friendly against Kilmarnock, pitching in all the youngsters I thought could make it. United won, 3–0.

The following Saturday, we were away to Huddersfield—they were going for the title—and I repeated the experiment. We drew, and we drew again, 2–2, in our next match, at home to Arsenal. So the gamble had begun. For the next couple of months I lived on a knife-edge, knowing that while we were getting reasonable results, this new-look team still had to show that it had knitted together.

All the time, I was telling the young players to enjoy themselves, to play their natural game, to concentrate on serving up good football. Results, I said, were not all-important. It was a massive confidence-building operation on my part—and, unknown to anyone, MY confidence was the most doubtful ingredient!

But after one especially impressive display by the

BELOW: TITLE WINNERS, season 1951–52. Back row (left to right): Manager Matt Busby, Jackie Blanchflower, John Aston, Reg. Allen, Allenby Chilton, Don Gibson, Henry Cockburn, Tom Curry (trainer). Front row: Stan Pearson, Jack Rowley, Johnny Carey, Johnny Downie, Harry McShane.

youngsters, I relaxed, and became convinced that inside two years we would have a title-winning side again. We finished fourth, and looked ahead to real success.

But what about the men who had been the first to put United on the map?—They deserved con-sideration, as well.

I like to think that United's treatment of those men laid the foundations for a policy that has generally become accepted over the years—that the Old Trafford club always does its best for people who have been good servants.

Allenby Chilton was allowed to join Grimsby as player-manager, and we didn't ask a fee; Jack Rowley became player-manager at Plymouth, again without fee; Johnny Carey had our blessing when he was offered the manager's job at Blackburn; and Jimmy Delaney, keen to return to Scotland, got his wish with a transfer to Aberdeen. So, with these amicable partings, we showed that there could be sentiment in football.

As for Manchester United, we began to make solid progress with our 'new' team. In 1953 we finished eighth, then we came fourth, then fifth. And in two successive seasons after that—1955–56 and 1956–57—United carried off the League championship. The players who had been dubbed the Busby Babes had arrived.

Progress had been made in many other directions, too, for the £15,000 debt of 1945 had been eliminated, crowds were approaching 40,000 regularly when we played at Old Trafford, and we were drawing the fans away from home. By 1957 the club had been able to spend in the region of £200,000 to rebuild the blitz-battered shell of a football ground and install the costliest floodlighting system in the country. More than that, the bank balance compared favourably with that of any other club in the land.

It hadn't all been achieved overnight, and it wasn't all the doing of Matt Busby. I had been given tremendous help by an able and loyal staff—Jimmy Murphy in particular—and between us we had grafted to ensure that, while the established team of the late 1940s was making headline news, behind the scenes United had secured some outstanding young talent which cost the club nothing.

Despite the old story about shouting down a mine shaft and seeing a footballer come up, the business of finding players is one of never-ending work, involving constant travel, careful scrutinising . . . and persuasive talking. Footballers don't grow on trees, and when you do find one who looks like making the grade, you know that you're not on your own. Other clubs are often fierce rivals for the lad's signature.

In the early days, a railway timetable was my constant companion, as I travelled the length and breadth of Britain to watch schoolboy sides, youth teams, works teams, even water-board teams. United had their scouting net out, and it was my job to follow up the tips of those scouts, regardless of the time involved or the distance to be covered.

Right from the start, too, I had made the decision

JOE ARMSTRONG, for many years Manchester United's chief scout, and the man who brought many of the potential stars to Old Trafford.

that only the best would be good enough for Manchester United. I wanted ability beyond question; I also wanted loyalty to myself and the club, players of real character, and lads who would be amenable to discipline, for without that you are headed for trouble.

It has often been said that Matt Busby ruled United with a velvet glove . . . but, while I never willingly washed dirty linen in public, as they say, I will add that there were times when I showed the glove could conceal an iron fist. I shall have more to say about this later.

Backing me to the hilt were the directors, and men such as Jimmy Murphy, Joe Armstrong, Tom Curry, Bert Whalley and Ted Dalton—and in my early days at Old Trafford there was Louis Rocca, then chief scout, whose contribution to the club's success can never be under-estimated. I always felt it was a tragedy that Louis didn't live to see United's memorable years of the late 1950s.

BUSBY BABES

FAR left, Jimmy Murphy — Matt Busby's right-hand man through the years; left, Jackie Blanchflower, who tried accountancy and plumbing, but admitted: 'All I want is to play football'. Below, Joe Mercer (inset), who gave Matt Busby a tip about Duncan Edwards.

BARI, in southern Italy, was where I first met Jimmy Murphy. It was wartime, and I was in charge of an Army football team playing exhibition matches for the troops. Jimmy and I established such a firm friendship that I promised him I would send for him, once I had achieved my aim of landing a managerial job, when peacetime football resumed. I kept my word, and Jimmy arrived at Old Trafford as assistant manager about a year after I had taken charge.

For many years, Jimmy and I shared the club's secrets and worked together, checking out players, discussing possible signings, mulling over the progress made and the way we wanted things to go. And although he could have taken a job elsewhere as a manager in his own right—not once, but time and again—he stayed with United and, even after he had officially retired, he kept us posted about players who might be the type we wanted.

It was Jimmy who took charge after the Munich air disaster in 1958, and who made decisions and signed players as United, somehow, fought through to reach the final of the F.A. Cup. When I came out of hospital, I was still hobbling on crutches as I visited the team at their pre-Wembley training headquarters at Blackpool, and it was good to see Jimmy's smiling face and know he had matters in hand.

Bert Whalley was another who did much to help the club. He had played for United at centre-half, without ever having established a regular first-team place, but his heart was at Old Trafford, and when an eye injury forced him to quit playing, he joined the staff.

When I was playing for Manchester City, Joe Armstrong was scouting for them: I didn't forget the shrewd job he had done at Maine-road, and he eventually landed at Old Trafford, to discover more potential star players than any of us. Joe worked for years, watched all manner of games in all kinds of weather—and seldom made a mistake about a youngster.

He was a retired civil servant, and his diplomatic manner was often a key factor when he talked to parents about letting their lads join United. He headed a team of eight scouts, and between them they turned up trumps. One of them, Bob Bishop, was the man responsible for finding George Best and Sammy McIlroy—the last of the so-called Busby Babes.

David Pegg was a Doncaster boy who, even in the England schools side, was outstanding. Norman Scholes, Bert Whalley and finally Jimmy Murphy watched him for United, and when he was ready to leave school, clubs were queueing to sign the lad. I decided to make a personal call on David's parents, and was not surprised to be told by his father that United were not the first club to have made an approach.

Mr. Pegg made it clear he was prepared to talk to every First Division club manager before the big decision was made, for above all he wanted to feel the lad had gone to the right place. He told me: 'I've always believed David has the ability to make himself a future in football . . . but what's your opinion, Mr. Busby? 'If there are any doubts, I'd rather he went in for another job, because I'm determined my boy will never do what I do for a living'. David's dad was down the pit.

I didn't try to gild the lily. I simply said: 'With reasonable luck, David will be successful as a

THREE of the Busby babes . . . left to right, David Pegg, Bobby Charlton and Liam Whelan. All of them became internationals, as did Tommy Taylor (right), signed from Barnsley after a cloak-and-dagger quest.

professional footballer. That is my opinion, and I don't think I'll be far out.' I like to think my honesty, and my avoidance of making extravagant promises, influenced Mr. Pegg's decision to let David join United. Tragically, David was one of the fine young players whose career ended prematurely on a snowswept airstrip at Munich.

Duncan Edwards was another Munich victim, and this young giant became a United player although he lived at Dudley, right on the doorstep of Wolves, whose manager, Stan Cullis, had been keeping a close watch on Duncan. Wolves were not the only other club wanting to sign the lad, but we found we had the trump card, in the end . . . Duncan's own, almost fanatical, keenness on Manchester United.

Stan Cullis once asked me, after Duncan had given

a five-star display against Wolves, how we had managed to land him. 'We thought he was all lined up to join Wolves,' said Stan. I answered: 'I got Duncan the same way you got Colin Booth (a Manchester lad). I was with Colin's parents the night before he joined Wolves. He was supposed to be joining United—but I don't hold that against you, Stan.' Booth just wanted to go to Wolves; Duncan chose United.

We lost one lad, Ray Parry, to Bolton, and another—Joe Dean—also went to Burnden Park. His father wanted him to join United, his mother thought the competition for a first-team place as goalkeeper would be too hot at Old Trafford. So Joe joined Bolton. From which it can be seen that you don't win 'em all.

Sometimes you make a mistake, too, as I did about a boy called Eric Bell, an inside-forward who, I felt, wouldn't quite measure up to our demands. I released him as an amateur, he went to Bolton—and became a very good wing-half.

I had my doubts about Jackie Blanchflower, too. His parents were convinced he would become a top-class player, and I persevered . . . though my patience was sorely tried. Initially, I backed the judgment of Irish scout Bob Harper, but during his first two months at Old Trafford Jackie was like a clam—you could barely get more than a 'Yes' or a 'No' out of him, and I worried over this apparently introverted character.

Finally, I dragged from him one fact—that he fancied becoming a chartered accountant. So we fixed him up as an articled clerk. Then one day he came to see me, apparently with the cares of the world on his young shoulders. 'I don't want to be an accountant any more, boss,' he said. When I asked if he had an alternative in mind, he answered: 'I could try my hand as a plumber.' We arranged for him to become an apprentice plumber.

Meanwhile, whether at inside-forward or at wing-half, he wasn't pulling up any trees as a footballer. On the ball, he was good; but he badly needed speeding up. He wanted to play the game at his pace, and that just wasn't good enough for First Division standards. Then, to cap it all, he told me he didn't think he was 'cut out to be a plumber.'

So I told him matters had to be thrashed out, and he looked at me, obviously unhappy about how his next words would be taken—and blurted out: 'All I want to do is play football . . . nothing else interests me.' So we concentrated on that.

Even then, at 17, he couldn't add those few, vital yards to his speed, and by this time I was so worried I decided to invite Jackie's parents over for a talk. His dad told me: 'We're not concerned about the way he has been struggling here—we know that if he doesn't make the grade at United, he could never become a footballer with any team.'

That showdown meeting proved a turning point, and Jackie set about proving he COULD make it with United—to such good effect that when he was switched to centre-half his progress was so swift he became an Irish international in a short time. Indeed, I then had the problem of keeping him happy because he couldn't get into our first team, despite the blinders he was having in the reserves. But, of course, he did finally break through.

'Snakehips' Eddie Colman was a Salford lad, and when I visited his parents, father and son surprised me by their attitude. Eddie seemed to have the impression he was picked for the Salford side to make up the numbers, and his dad didn't appear to regard him as a sought-after starlet, either. Mr. Colman put it this way: 'All I want is a future for my son. If you're sure he has a future as a footballer, he can certainly join United.' I was sure—and he did.

The Tommy Taylor story? He was making his name with Barnsley, when he wasn't starring for an Army side, and I knew he was what we needed. He was also wanted by several other clubs. I told my board: 'You can write off at least £30,000, if we are to get Taylor.'

That was a lot of money then, and my board could easily have said it was too much. Yet chairman Harold Hardman and his fellow-directors said: 'If you think he's worth that money, Matt, go out and get him.' Easier said than done . . .

Barnsley had offers from clubs such as Cardiff, Chelsea, Manchester City, Sunderland and West Brom. At £20,000 one or two dropped out; at £25,000, the field was narrowed further. But three clubs were still ready to go to £30,000, and United were one of them.

Jimmy Murphy and I went to stay in Barnsley; so did Cardiff boss Cyril Spiers. We stayed four days and nights, wondering all the time if Cyril was stealing a march on us, and the tension strained our nerves so much that I said to Jimmy: 'Let's forget Cyril Spiers and Tommy Taylor for a couple of hours—we'll go to the pictures.'

Jimmy tipped the usherette two half-crowns and told her: 'If a tall man wearing a camel coat comes in, let me know.' Cyril Spiers had a liking for that type of coat . . . and soon afterwards the usherette tapped Jimmy's arm and shone her torch on Cyril as she guided him to a seat not far from us!

The chase finally ended when Barnsley chairman Joe Richards told me in his office: 'The fee for Tommy Taylor is £30,000. Pay that, and he's yours.' I answered: 'Big fees have affected players in the past; that £30,000 tag could easily ruin Taylor, if it preyed on his mind.' And I offered . . . £29,999. The offer was accepted.

But then Tommy told me: 'I'm not keen to leave Barnsley, and I don't think I'll sign yet'. He asked for six weeks' grace, giving me a promise that if he didn't join United, he wouldn't go elsewhere.

IN action for United . . . Harry Gregg, a world-record signing at £23,500. Right, winger Johnny Berry gets a spot of treatment from physio Ted Dalton. Berry was signed from Birmingham.

I told the lad he was shirking the issue, that six weeks hence he would still have to make the decision. I struck just the right note, for he said: 'Pass me the pen, Mr. Busby . . .' And so Tommy signed.

Towards the end of 1957, United paid what was then a world-record fee for a goalkeeper, Harry Gregg, who played for Doncaster Rovers. The price was £23,500. And we just beat Sheffield Wednesday to the punch. It was said that Wednesday had offered £18,000 and, as far as the newspapers were concerned, they were going to get their man even if they had to go higher to land him.

United were also in the hunt, but I was playing it close to my chest—until, on the Saturday night, a newspaper reporter rang me at home and persisted in asking for a straight answer to a straight question. 'Have you made an offer for Harry Gregg?'

I realised there was no way I could get round the subject without telling an outright lie, and finally admitted United's interest. But I didn't rest easy that night, knowing the story was out.

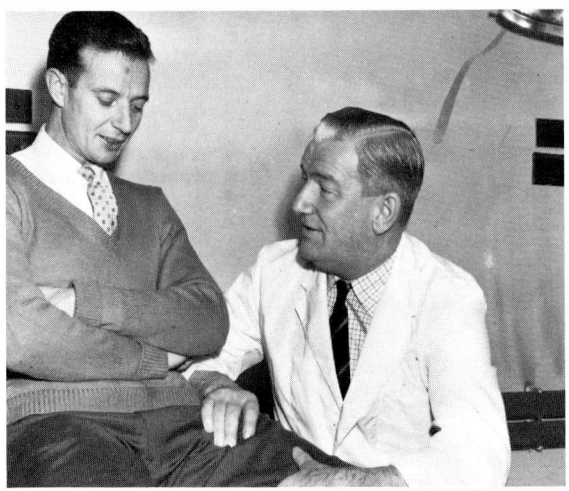

The transfer deal was concluded in an atmosphere of secrecy. Harry reported for training, and was told to return to the ground at 2.30 p.m. A club official took him by car—Harry wasn't put in the picture at that stage—and they arrived at the home of Doncaster manager Peter Doherty. The transfer forms were waiting.

When reporters were spotted near the house, Harry dodged down on the floor below window level, then the curtains were drawn . . . and not until I walked into the room did Harry Gregg know which club it was.

Harry Gregg gave United 10 years' service as a player. Then, 20 years after having first signed for the club, he came back, after a career in management, to give us the benefit of his knowledge on the coaching side.

Jimmy Delaney's departure left a gap on the right wing, and although we had youngsters coming through, this was one position I felt must be filled by an experienced player. Since there was no obvious candidate at the club for the job, Johnny Berry of Birmingham became my target; and with good reason. Every time he played against United, he seemed to put one across us.

One season, with 10 games to go, we were four points clear at the top, and Birmingham were in the relegation zone . . . but at Old Trafford on the Good Friday, Berry played a key role as they took two precious points from us. Once, he took the ball from his own 18-yard box, beat man after man as he sped down the field, feinted to make a pass, spurted ahead—and unleashed a tremendous shot which almost broke the net.

On the Easter Monday in the return game, he was outstanding again. So I decided to apply a new twist to the old motto—if you can't beat 'em, get them to join you. But Birmingham were not of the same mind, when it came to parting with Berry, and he was still having a field day against us the following season. I kept asking about him, Birmingham kept telling me they wouldn't let him go. Then one day manager Bob Brocklebank rang me to say: 'The board have agreed to sell Berry. But no haggling. The price is £25,000.'

My answer: 'I'm on my way.' I didn't even check on the train times . . . Jimmy Murphy and I were driving away from Old Trafford within 10 minutes of that call, and five minutes after I met Johnny Berry, he was a United player.

So, as a manager, I won some and I lost some. In fact, once I lost a player and gained another, thanks to Joe Mercer, whom I had asked about a youngster from Joe's home town of Hoylake. Joe told me: 'You haven't a chance—the lad is Everton-daft, and I think he's bound for Goodison.' He was—but later Joe said to me: 'I don't know why you were concerned about that lad in the England boys team . . . the best of the bunch is a 14-year-old giant. He'll make a world-beater.'

That lad was Duncan Edwards, and that was how we started on his trail. When I finally asked him to join United, Duncan said: 'I think they're the greatest club in the world. I'd give anything to play for your team.' And after he had arrived at Old Trafford, I remember how, having given the new boys a talk one day, I took Jimmy Murphy on one side and said: 'All the time I've been talking, the big lad in the corner (Edwards) has had his eyes on me, taking everything in.' Duncan was a quick learner. He was playing for the full England side while still in his teens.

Now and again, you pick a loser. One lad on the ground staff wasn't so eager to learn. A week after joining us, he went missing on the Monday morning, and the following day offered this excuse: 'I was too tired to turn up.' I gave him a warning, but a week later he played truant again.

It was clear he wasn't prepared to take his job seriously, that he lacked discipline. I sent him home, and that was that. Maybe I was sacking a future international, but I was ready to take the risk rather than have that lad's attitude infect other more conscientious players.

CONTROVERSY and the F.A. Cup have often been close companions, and Manchester United figured in one of the most controversial Wembley finals in 1957 on a day which began with my feeling convinced that we would hammer Aston Villa into submission. We were already League champions, 90 minutes away from the double which had last been achieved 60 years previously by . . . Aston Villa.

I considered the Villa side of that day to be strong, especially in defence, but not clever: though in my team talk I had warned of the danger Northern Ireland—international winger Peter McParland could spell.

In the week before the final, I had worried about injuries to players, especially one to Jackie Blanchflower, but he was in the line-up on the big day and destined to play a totally different role from the one I had envisaged. So was McParland.

Only six minutes had gone by when United's 'keeper, Ray Wood, was being helped from the field, his cheek bone smashed. And Jackie was taking over in goal.

It had all stemmed from what seemed such a simple thing—McParland had headed the ball, Ray Wood had caught it cleanly. As the 'keeper was pondering where to kick the ball, McParland bore down on goal and hurled himself at Wood, who went down as if pole-axed. Ray came back to make fleeting appearances on the wing, though he was constantly suffering from blackouts; for 84 minutes it was effectively 10 men against 11.

At half-time, the score was still 0–0, but despite goalkeeping heroics from Blanchflower and a headed goal by Tommy Taylor, United's resistance had to crumble, and McParland hit two goals to ensure that the Cup went to Villa. Afterwards, I heard a remark that 'McParland got two goals and a goalkeeper',

Wood hadn't been standing on the goal line—then, a charge might have produced a legitimate goal. Neither had he been fumbling with the ball—in which case a charge might have caused him to lose it. The way it happened, the ball was secure in his hands, and United were in no danger. But that inexplicable action by McParland changed the whole complexion of the game almost at the outset.

Yet there was one moment of comedy, which only emphasised the tragic aspect of things, from United's point of view. At half-time physiotherapist Ted Dalton took Ray to the rear of the stadium and tested the 'keeper by throwing and kicking a ball to him. As

they went through the charade—Ray could see no more than a couple out of every half-dozen balls sent to him—on a deserted grass strip outside the packed ground, a cockney kid who had turned up to watch the performance told the 'keeper: 'Look, mister. My mates and me have got a game on just round the corner. You can come and play with us, if you like.'

The following year, Manchester United returned to Wembley . . . but if the McParland-Wood incident had made news around the country, what had happened between the two finals had made headlines world-wide. In February 1958 Manchester United's team had been virtually decimated by the air crash at Munich.

We were returning from a European tie in Belgrade, and the next item on the agenda was to have been an F.A. Cup battle with Sheffield Wednesday. I knew nothing about what was going on, since I lay close to death in a Munich hospital, but I learned the details later and I was able to be at Wembley when United had achieved what appeared to be mission impossible . . . reaching the F.A. Cup final.

The burden of carrying on fell squarely on the shoulders of Jimmy Murphy, and he wasted no time in taking action. Players were dead, others were dying or still gravely ill, but—somehow— the club had to carry on. This meant that reinforcements must be recruited, and swiftly; so, almost overnight, men like Ernie Taylor and Stan Crowther were signed from Blackpool and Aston Villa respectively, and youngsters whose names were barely known outside Old Trafford were given the responsibility of filling the boots of household names.

Crowther signed for United a matter of hours before the Cup-tie against Sheffield Wednesday at Old Trafford, and 60,000 people flocked to the stadium to see what the new-look Manchester United could achieve. The pre-Munich side had disposed of Workington and Derby County; now it was up to the new boys.

Wednesday were fighting not just a team of 11 players but the will of the crowd that night, and United were inspired to an emotional victory.

West Brom were despatched in the sixth round, and that meant a semi-final against Fulham. I imagine that outside the hard core of fans who supported West Brom and Fulham, the rest of the country was on the side of United, who were carried along on a crescendo of sound and sentiment. United

CONTROVERSY AND THE F.A. CUP

held Fulham to a draw, won the replay, and by the time the players were toning up at Blackpool a week before the final—against Bolton—I was able to hobble along and be with them.

I was determined to be at Wembley, despite advice that it would be better for me if I didn't make the tiring trip. But I had made up my mind. Frankly, I couldn't have told anyone what I expected to see in this final, because I knew there must be a limit to the number of times a team can raise its game and finish in triumph. United had already excelled themselves in knocking out Wednesday, West Brom and Fulham . . . who knew how they would fare against Bolton in the final itself?

So I thought I was prepared for anything—but I was NOT prepared for another incident involving Manchester United's goalkeeper. This time it wasn't Ray Wood, but Harry Gregg, one of the survivors from Munich.

There were three other Munich men in the team— Bobby Charlton, Dennis Viollet and Bill Foulkes— and there was the added experience of Ernie Taylor and Stan Crowther, who had been in Villa's Cup-final side against United the previous year.

There were also the 'rookies' . . . Colin Webster, Ronnie Cope, Alex Dawson, Freddie Goodwin and Ian Greaves, although Freddie and Ian had sampled First Division football more than the others. However, Bolton's side was packed with experience . . . Eddie Hopkinson, Roy Hartle, Tommy Banks, Derek Hennin, John Higgins, Brian Edwards, Brian Birch, Dennis Stevens, Ray Parry, Doug Holden and—at centre-forward—England's Nat Lofthouse.

So it could be a case of the men against the boys, and I recognised in particular the menace of Lofthouse, a powerful, fearless striker who could bulldoze his way through a defence which might be at all hesitant. In fact, it was Lofthouse who scored Bolton's two goals which won the Cup for them—and Lofthouse who figured in the final's controversial incident.

In the second half, a Bolton forward hit the ball goalwards, and Gregg went up and tried to push the ball over the bar. The ball hit his hand and spun in the air, dropping just short of the bar. The 'keeper twisted round to grab the ball, facing the crowd and catching a glimpse of a sea of faces. As Harry Gregg said afterwards, the next thing he knew, he was being doused with water by trainer Jack Crompton.

Lofthouse had gone in with the hope of scoring, but had caught the 'keeper, who went down and lay writhing on the ground. Was it a fair shoulder charge or—as United's 'keeper maintained—a thump in the back? The arguments raged afterwards, but the scoreline still said Bolton 2, Manchester United 0.

Well, things like this happen in football, and though it was a tremendous disappointment to have lost in successive finals, I felt proud of the way my team had aquitted itself after such a tragedy as Munich. Nevertheless, as my own fitness gradually improved, I knew that once again I had to take stock and set about rebuilding, for my sights were still on the European Cup, as well as honours at home.

United had scored an aggregate 5–4 victory over Red Star Belgrade in the European tie immediately preceding Munich, and I still believe that but for the air crash we would have gone on to the final and ultimate triumph that year. As it was, another decade went by before we achieved the burning ambition . . . and then, in 1968, the stage was Wembley.

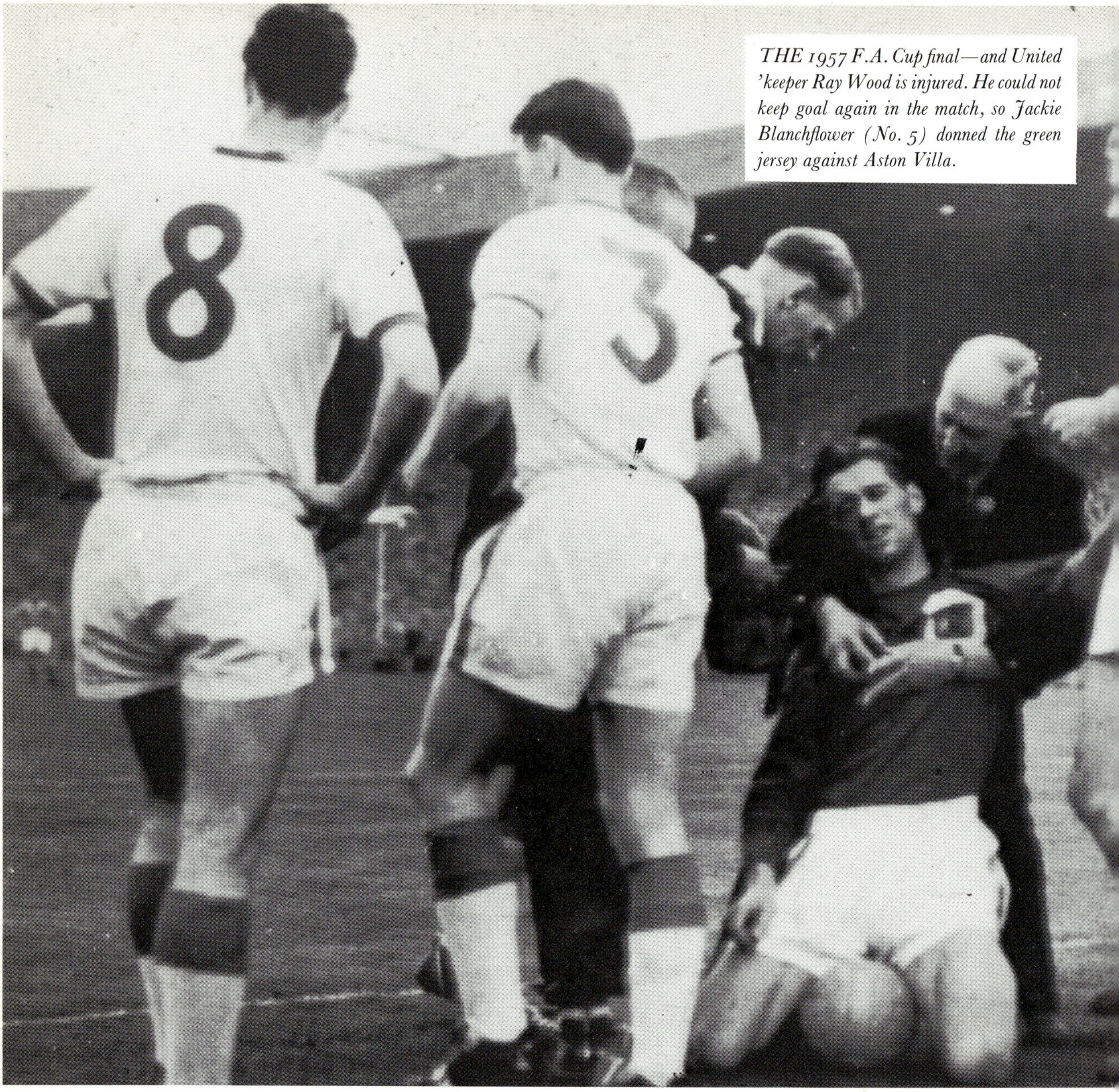

THE 1957 F.A. Cup final—and United 'keeper Ray Wood is injured. He could not keep goal again in the match, so Jackie Blanchflower (No. 5) donned the green jersey against Aston Villa.

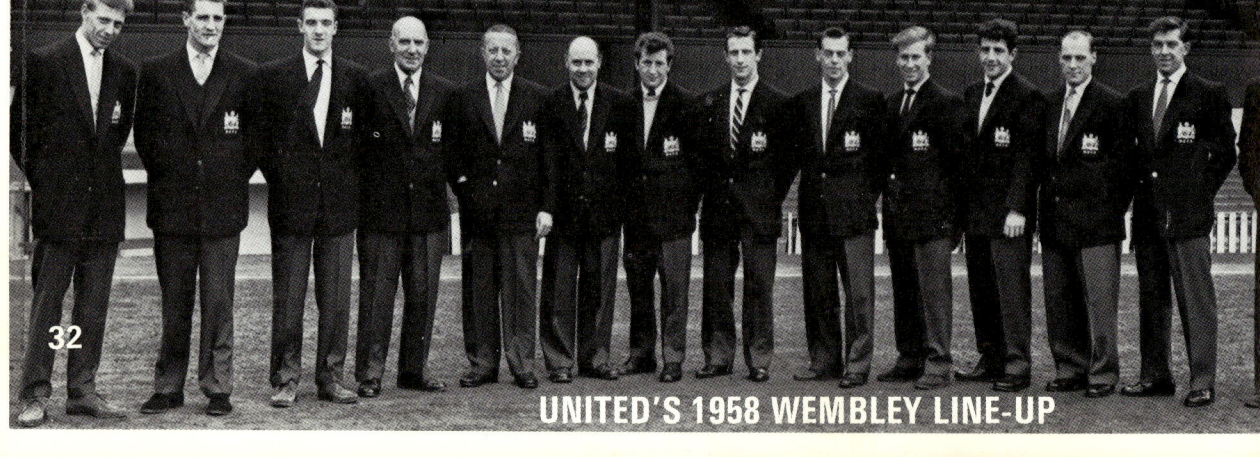

UNITED'S 1958 WEMBLEY LINE-UP

DOUBLE DRAMA AT WEMBLEY

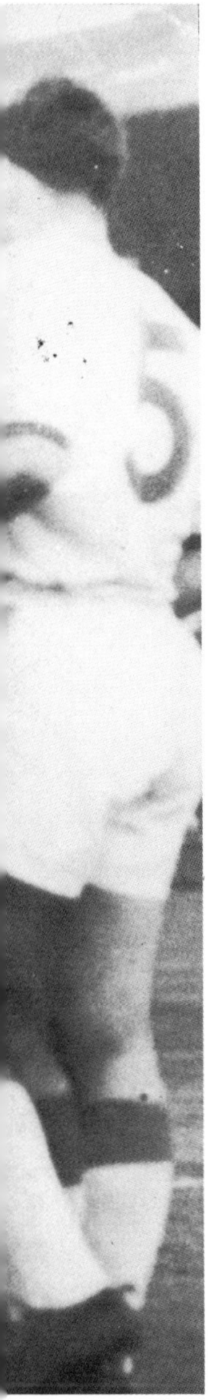

THE 1958 F.A. Cup final—and this time it's United 'keeper Harry Gregg taking the knock, as Bolton centre-forward Nat Lofthouse crashes into him after heading for goal. Below, Gregg is out cold, the ball is in the net. Lofthouse scored two goals, Bolton claimed the Cup.

ENCOUNTERS WITH REAL MADRID

THROUGH the years, United have met, matched—even mastered—Real Madrid, the original Kings of Europe, who won the European Cup five successive times. United conquered Real in the 1968 semi-final on their way to ultimate triumph. Right, Real with replicas of their five trophies; below, United salute the fans in Real's Bernabeu stadium; bottom picture, the Real side of 1957—back row (left to right): Alonso, Becerril, Marquitos, Lesmes, Munoz, Zarraga. Front row: Kopa, Mateos, Di Stefano, Rial, Gento.

34

LEFT, Real president Santiago Bernabeu presents United chairman Harold Hardman with a statuette, after the game in Madrid in 1957; below, Denis Law and Gento lead out the teams at Old Trafford for the first leg of the 1968 European Cup semi-final.

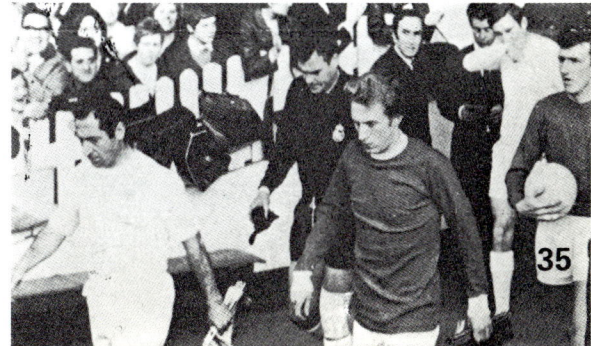

SEASON 1956–57 saw Manchester United embarking for the first time on the quest for the European Cup. We were to learn many lessons before we finally triumphed, in 1968, but we began with a rousing, first-round win against Belgian champions Anderlecht. After beating them 2–0 in Brussels, United hammered 10 goals past them in the return, which was played under the lights at Maine-road, since Old Trafford was still being restored after the war damage.

Borussia Dortmund lost 3–0 in Manchester and could only draw, 0–0, in Germany, and this brought us up against Bilbao. I went to watch them. Bilbao had won their home leg 3–2 against Honved, but because of troubles in Hungary the second leg was played in Brussels. Bilbao scored in the first few minutes, Honved had a succession of injury problems, and three-quarters of the way through the game my money was on Bilbao.

They were 3–1 up, Honved's 'keeper had been carried off, Czibor was limping . . . so it looked like United versus Bilbao. But when Puskas and Kocsis scored, to make it 3–3, I began to wonder, especially as the Honved forwards were buzzing round Bilbao's goal like bees. The challenge, however, had been left too late, and the referee's whistle came to Bilbao's rescue, so it meant that we would take on the team from Spain after all.

Bilbao played their football like an English team—they were quick on the ball, direct in attacking strategy, bent on going for goal. It would be like playing Wolves, I felt. And instead of sunshine when we travelled to Spain, it could have been an evening during mid-season in England: snow followed days of torrential rain, so that the quagmire of a pitch turned white.

By half-time the Basques were leading 3–0, and United were looking a beaten side. Yet we hit back to make it 3–2 . . . then Bilbao struck a fourth goal . . . and a fifth. It was then that Liam Whelan scored one of the best—and most valuable—goals I have seen, as he ploughed his way half the length of the field, taking on and beating men, and as he reached a spot where I was muttering to myself, 'Hit it now, hit it now!' he still carried on a few yards—then, as the Bilbao 'keeper stood, seemingly mesmerised, the Irishman planted the ball past him.

We had to be back in time to play a League game against Sheffield Wednesday on the Saturday, and a blizzard threatened to delay our departure from

THE LESSONS LEARNED IN

Spain. At the airport players, club officials and Pressmen buckled to, using brooms to sweep snow and ice from the wings of the two planes waiting to carry us home. We made it, and prepared for the return leg of the European tie at Maine-road.

Quite simply, United needed to win 3–0 to ensure success; and that was a tall order. We needed the encouragement of every single fan, and utter dedication from the players. From the moment United appeared, the atmosphere was electric, and for 90 solid minutes those fans never stopped urging us on. They were rewarded by seeing United find the net twice, and have the goals disallowed—yet still score the three goals the situation demanded.

It was just before half time when Dennis Viollet struck the first. Then, after half-time, came those two disallowed goals; and, at last, the breakthrough, when Tommy Taylor gave centre-half Garay the slip and crashed an unstoppable shot home, to make the scoreline 5–5 overall.

With fewer than 10 minutes to go, Johnny Berry—the man who, so often, had tormented us when he was wearing Birmingham's colours—did the trick and became United's scoring hero, though every man in the side had performed heroics. We were through to the semi-finals at our first attempt.

We were paired with Real or Nice, and since Real held a comfortable first-leg lead, I flew to Nice anticipating the worst. My fears were justified; we had to take on what was recognised as the greatest side in Europe. Real had world-class stars such as Di Stefano, Gento, Kopa, Marquitos, and they had won the European Cup by beating Rheims 4–3 in the final in Paris the previous season. They were to accomplish the fantastic feat of claiming the trophy five years in a row, too.

The first leg of the semi-final was in Madrid, and the ticket spivs made a fortune. We had a scare 24 hours before the game when Liam Whelan—we all called him Billy—had a bad nose bleed during a training session, and we smuggled him back to the hotel, in an effort to keep this problem a secret. The doctor said he would be fit to play, providing there

THAT UNITED EUROPE . . .

was no recurrence of the nose-bleed, and on the day of the match I was relieved when I knew I could name Billy in United's line-up.

Thirty minutes before kick-off time I had a shock when Real Madrid officials knocked on the dressing-room door and handed to me eleven portraits of their players, so that I could check they were fielding the men they had named—and then they demanded: 'Now, your pictures, please'.

I said we hadn't got any, and that F.I.F.A. rules made no such demands. They suggested we were not playing fair, hinted that the game could be postponed if we didn't comply with their request. I told them: 'When we get back to the hotel after the game, you can see the players' passports. That's the best I can do.' They weren't happy, but didn't prolong the argument.

And the match? For 45 minutes it was purely a holding operation by United, as Real attacked. Yet even Di Stefano came in for abuse from his own fans as he failed to find a way through. Every time he got the ball, Eddie Colman or Jackie Blanchflower was there, shadowing him and, usually, winning possession. The great man became so frustrated that, completely out of character, he put in one tackle on Blanchflower which looked vicious.

It was 0–0 at half-time, even though Bill Foulkes had been run dizzy by Gento, and the forwards—probably unnerved by the occasion—had scarcely been seen.

The second half saw Real take command in quick time as Rial headed a left-wing cross past Ray Wood; and at last Di Stefano won cheers from his fans as he collected a pass on the half-way line, raced through our defence, drew Wood out of goal and lobbed a 25-yarder over the 'keeper and into the net.

Our forwards finally awoke to the situation, and during a spell of pressure Taylor scored. But Real made it 3–1 when Mateos ran 30 yards with the ball before slipping a shot past Wood.

So, at the end, it was a question of whether or not United could do what they had done against Bilbao . . . wipe out a two-goal deficit. And, as has happened countless times in European games since, an element of gamesmanship entered into the scheme of things.

Ten days before the return, Real—having decided that they were not going to risk Becerril getting a chasing from David Pegg such as had happened during the late stages of the first match—signed a right-back named Torres on loan from Zaragoza 'until the end of the season'.

I wondered whether to protest to F.I.F.A.—but found that Real had taken the precaution of including the name Torres in their provisional list of players for the match, and within the time limit required. So he was eligible, all right. The Spaniards had worked a smart, flanking move, but it was legal.

Now, it is also legal to water the pitch to a certain extent, and—since United liked a heavy ground—I ordered constant use of the sprinklers on the Old Trafford ground. However, I hadn't bargained for a photographer taking a picture, and when it appeared on the morning of the game it gave the idea that we had undertaken a flooding operation, since pools of water were visible. In fact, the water simply hadn't had time to soak into the turf.

A deputation from Real arrived at Old Trafford and asked what game we were playing. Their ultimatum: 'Turn off the sprinklers, or we don't play today.' And they would not rest until we assured them that the tap would be turned off.

It made no difference, on the night. Kopa, Gento and Di Stefano turned it on—the brilliant football, I mean—and by half-time United were trailing 2–0, and 5–1 on aggregate. We scored twice after the restart, but we couldn't really hope to wipe out a four-goal deficit in 45 minutes.

Real had done their homework and got their sums right. They had realised that Bilbao's attitude of 'what we have, we hold' had got them into trouble at Maine-road in the previous round. So Real had decided to nail us as soon as possible. That was another lesson I learned from our first encounter with the great Spanish club.

At the time, I said that Real defeated United because a great, experienced side would always triumph over a great, inexperienced side. The average age of the Real players was 28, the average age of the United players around 21.

I added that, while I did not normally go in for rash forecasting, I believed that if United met Real in a couple of years, the game would go in our favour. It took longer than a couple of years, but we made it.

ITALY, SPAIN?—I COULD HAVE BECOME A WEALTHY MAN . . .

WE have become accustomed to the idea of players from Europe signing for British clubs and players from this country opting for careers in Europe. But close on 20 years before Kevin Keegan went to S.V. Hamburg the trail was blazed by a few stars. John Charles left Leeds United for Juventus and the sunshine of Italy, and when England played Denmark in Copenhagen in 1957, the Italian clubs were represented in force.

I was there, and it soon became clear that at least one club had designs on the man I had bought from Barnsley for £29,999. Tommy Taylor's display for England had impressed the Italians, and they made it plain to me that if I would allow Tommy to move into Italian football, Manchester United could console themselves with a very large sum of lire.

Leeds had allowed Charles to go, Tottenham had given Tony Marchi, their England half-back, the chance to move, and perhaps you might think I should have followed the same line, which was that it would be unfair to prevent a player cashing in on his undoubted ability. But I believed there was a much broader issue at stake—the future of my club.

Tommy Taylor wasn't the only star—not even the major star—in the constellation at Old Trafford. If he went, it would surely open the door for overtures from Italy for players such as Duncan Edwards, Billy Whelan, David Pegg, Jackie Blanchflower. Where, indeed, would it stop?

I foresaw the very real danger that the lure of the lire could bring about the demolition of Manchester United, or at least, the carving up of a team which had taken a great deal of time and trouble to assemble. A transfer to Italy for Tommy Taylor could have been the thin end of the wedge . . . and shattered what, to me, was my life's work.

So no business was done, although it was not for want of trying on the Italians' part. Tommy returned to his club, I flew to Zurich for a youth tournament . . . and there they were again, these persistent Italians. Not in Switzerland, but making an approach to the player himself while United's manager was out of the country.

I got to hear of the promises they were making: promises which could easily turn a young player's head and make him unable to see anything but the glitter of the lire in a land of permanent sunshine. The story even got about that Tommy himself had agreed to go to Italy.

On my return, I wasted no time in calling Tommy to my office and having a heart-to-heart with him. As a result, I quashed any possible idea of him leaving Old Trafford. I might have been hard on him, if you suggest that I stood in the way of his making a fortune; but to me, the well-being of Manchester United was paramount. It wasn't Matt Busby who mattered most—nor Tommy Taylor either.

The Taylor episode occurred in May 1957 . . . and that same month, there was another spate of rumours from Italy, to the effect that Matt Busby was the target, and that he was about to take up the job of managing the Italian international team at a salary of £100,000 a year.

Then it was reported that, having considered this munificent offer, I had decided against accepting it. The plain truth is that never was I offered such a sum, neither was it ever suggested to my face that I should go to Italy. And perhaps now you are asking . . . 'Ah, but what if it HAD been made?'

Let me say that I feel certain I would have turned it down. And that is not idle talk, or an attempt at whitewash, for in fact, I WAS asked to manage teams abroad—not once, but several times. Had I been

JIMMY GREAVES . . . one of half a dozen stars who moved abroad. Some stayed to find new fame, others decided that 'home' for them was the English League.

THE DAY UNITED REVERSED A TREND

level—'I felt deeply that I was in charge of the greatest football club in the world. That was sufficient reward for me . . . so what more could I want?

John Charles, Tony Marchi, Eddie Firmani, Gerry Hitchens, Jimmy Greaves, Joe Baker, Denis Law . . . these players all went to Italy. A few stayed to win new fame and, presumably, fortune; others found that the land of the lire left many things to be desired, so far as their footballing lives were concerned, and eventually they returned to English League Soccer.

There came a day in July 1962 when Manchester United played a part in reversing the trend, as they paid what was then regarded as a staggering sum of money—£115,000—to bring Denis Law *back* from Italy . . . and there were people who expressed the opinion that Matt Busby must have taken leave of his senses to spend such a vast amount of cash on one player.

In view of the kind of money which changed hands during the late 1970s, the Law fee now seems nothing more than commonplace; but at the time United's move was regarded as sensational.

There came another day when Denis himself was pushing Manchester United for improved terms, and I dug in my heels. Around that time, I had to go to Portugal for a European football meeting, and while I was in Estoril—naturally—the talk turned to United's current problems regarding Law.

Five of us were having dinner that night, and one member of the party expressed the view that the fee I had paid for Denis had been over the odds, in the first place, and that United would never really recoup all the cash.

I recall pointing out that Law had more than helped to pay for himself, not merely by his play and the goals he scored, but by his drawing power. 'He's helped to pay for a new stand, among other things,' I said.

That night none of us foresaw that the day would dawn when Denis would be given a free transfer from Old Trafford, and that he would return to Manchester City, the club which had first transferred him to Italy. But the Denis Law saga is another story.

inclined to think only about the money, I could have become a rich man two decades ago; but there was something about Manchester, and Manchester United, which made me determined to resist all the blandishments and stay loyal to the club.

I should add that among the offers I received was one from an Italian club, and it would not have been natural if I had dismissed the approach out of hand. I listened, out of courtesy; I also mentally listed the advantages (and they seemed numerous) and the disadvantages (which appeared to be few). And still I decided to stay put, just as I did when it was put to me that I should take my family to the United States and become one of the Soccer pioneers there.

As a matter of interest, Bilbao's defeat by Manchester United in the European Cup was followed not long afterwards by a decision on the part of the Spanish club to dispense with the services of their manager. And the new man they wanted? Matt Busby.

You can believe me when I say that Bilbao offered me terms which few men could have resisted—and I say that advisedly, knowing exactly HOW much money was involved. But again I stuck to my convictions that money isn't everything, and to this day I cannot say that I have ever regretted my decision.

To put it at its simplest—and also at its highest

MORE ABOUT THE BUSBY BABES

I HAVE already mentioned some of the players who became known as the Busby Babes. Jackie Blanchflower, David Pegg, Eddie Colman, Duncan Edwards . . . the names still roll off the tongue. There were others, too—Roger Byrne, Liam Whelan, Dennis Viollet, Bobby Charlton were from the same vintage crop.

Roger was playing at inside-forward for a boys' club team when Bert Whalley saw him, liked what he saw, and signed him as an amateur. Roger came to Old Trafford and stayed to become skipper of the first team—at left-back—and an England regular.

Billy Whelan literally arrived at United by accident: an accident which had put another player out of Manchester United's F.A. Youth Cup side. Dublin scout Billy Behan had tipped us off about Whelan, who was playing for the famous nursery club, Home Farm, but when I made a trip to Ireland it was with the idea of signing a player from League of Ireland club Waterford.

However, since they were not playing until the afternoon, I decided to take the opportunity of watching Whelan in a game that morning, and though he didn't touch the ball more than a dozen times, I liked what I saw.

Even so, United didn't rush in, because I felt that it would be wise to make further checks. We did so, and the reports kept on giving the youngster a good name. I started to ponder on whether we should invite him to Old Trafford for a trial.

Then John Doherty was injured, and ruled out of the F.A. Youth Cup final against Wolves. That made up my mind for me. I told Bert Whalley that Whelan might just be the player to do Doherty's job in the final. 'Go and watch him—if you think he's good enough, bring him back to Manchester with you,' was my parting shot.

Bert and Billy came back on the same plane, and the Irish lad made his debut in United's colours in that Youth Cup final. He clearly lacked pace, but he performed creditably enough, and that was the start of his career with United

Dennis Viollet was first recommended to me by Joe Armstrong. The lad had played for Manchester Schools and done well, and Joe fancied him strongly then. He fancied him even more when Dennis became the captain of the England schoolboy side. Yet there might have been a snag to Dennis becoming a United player . . . he lived near Maine-road, and his parents were Manchester City-minded.

But when we followed up a final check—made by Jimmy Murphy, Bert Whalley and myself—and went into the heart of City territory for a chat with the Viollet family, mother and father both seemed happy enough at the prospect of Dennis wearing the red jersey and not the blue one. So he was signed, and went on to play for England at senior level. Indeed, he became an international in a team of internationals . . . with some more internationals as reserves.

Mark Jones, who competed with Jackie Blanchflower for the centre-half position, came from Wombwell in Yorkshire. But he came to my attention when he played in an England schoolboy international trial right on the doorstep, for the game was staged at Old Trafford. Louis Rocca and Joe Armstrong kept a watching brief on Mark, and finally he returned to Old Trafford, this time to sign.

Bobby Charlton, of course, came from a famous footballing family up in the North-East, and when he first made an impression at United it was as a serious challenger to Dennis Viollet for the inside-left position. He showed that he could play in virtually any forward role, and as the years rolled by he matured to become one of the finest players ever to grace the jersey of England, as well as Manchester United.

During the late 1950s, I was concentrating my attention not merely on producing a first team of genuine quality—one to beat all the rest—but on ensuring that at Old Trafford there was an assembly line of talent for the future.

Waiting in the wings were youngsters such as David Gaskell—who, as a teenager, was pitched into a derby game against Manchester City when 'keeper Ray Wood went off injured—Peter Jones, Kenny Morgans, Albert Scanlon, Colin Webster, Mark Pearson, Bob English, Reg Holland, Barry Smith, Reg Hunter, Gordon Clayton and Wilf McGuinness.

I remember a top-of-the-table game at White Hart Lane against Tottenham on the Saturday after we had returned from a European tie in Germany. We had several injury worries, and I switched Duncan Edwards to the front line, handing Wilf the job of filling Duncan's boots at left-half.

In the first quarter of an hour, Tommy Harmer simply dazzled for Spurs, and they raced into a two-goal lead. From then on, Wilf stuck to Harmer like glue, and no more damage was done. United clawed their way back into the game and finished level.

SOCCER action—and Roger Byrne wins the ball, as Mark Jones (behind him) is ready to cover, should the need arise.

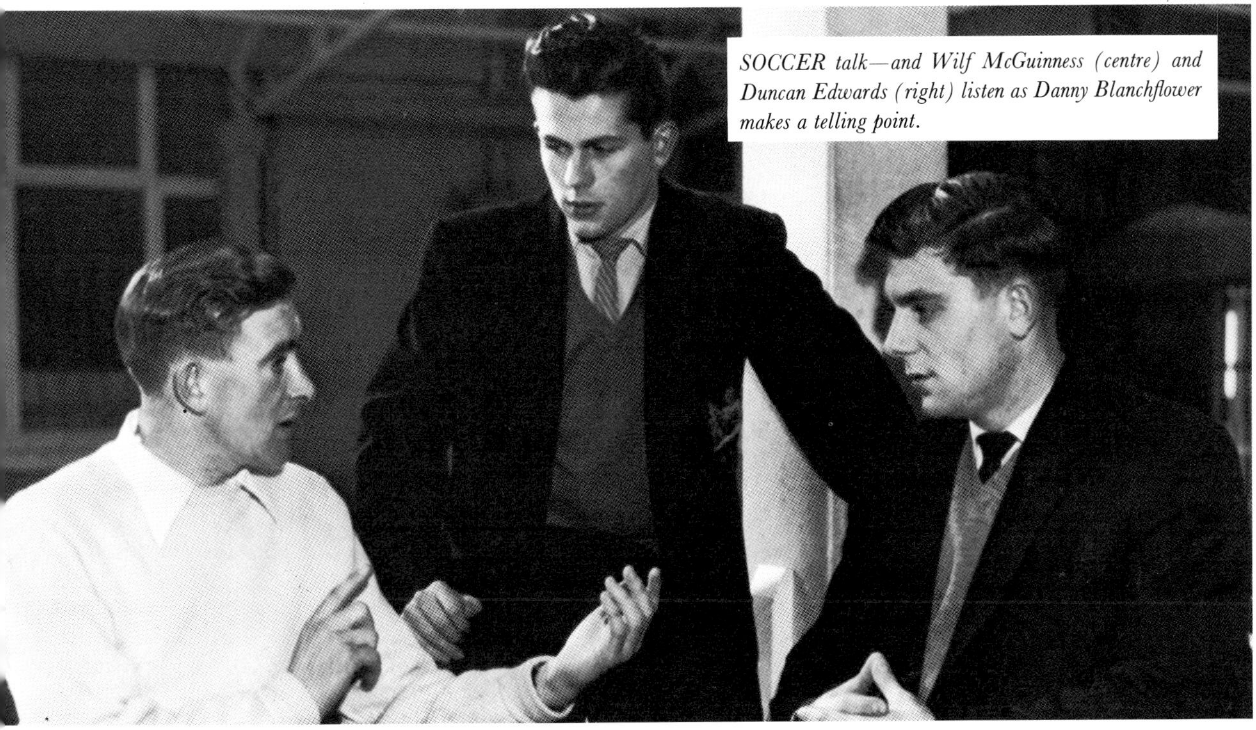

SOCCER talk—and Wilf McGuinness (centre) and Duncan Edwards (right) listen as Danny Blanchflower makes a telling point.

One Easter Monday I was able to field no fewer than eight of my reserve players in the first team against Burnley, and United scored a comfortable win . . . while on the same day, our Central League side (containing eight members of the youth team) went to Turf Moor and took two points from Burnley's reserves.

At that time United had a playing staff of 39, and 38 of them were under the age of 30, with many still in their teens or early 20s. Manchester United had had a monopoly on the F.A. Youth Cup, which they won five years on the trot, and thousands of fans rolled up to watch the reserves and the youngsters

Inevitably, not every lad blossomed into a star—

the wastage in professional football is considerable—but United proved that success could be built without having to spend a fortune in transfer fees. Indeed, whenever I did venture into the market, it was only after having assessed every player on the staff at Old Trafford and decided that, for this or that particular position, we didn't have the player to do the job. There might well have been a youngster who promised to make the breakthrough, in time, but even United could not afford to wait maybe two or three years, when one key signing could add the ingredient for continued success.

It was natural, also, that at times a youngster would knock on my office door and question his prospects of getting regular first-team football—after all, at one stage United had almost two teams of internationals on the books. My answer hardly ever varied. 'With all the commitments we have, you're wanted here—and you'll get your chance to play for the first team.' I doubt if there was a single lad who could turn round and say, in later years, that he was never given a chance at Old Trafford.

Munich destroyed a great team, and youngsters who were pitched into the side immediately afterwards were having to shoulder a great responsibility. Many of them grew up to become men almost overnight, and stayed to serve the club for years. Others, perhaps, found the adjustment too great to handle, and in time they were allowed to go to other clubs as United rebuilt in the effort to become the best in the business again.

Had the air disaster not happened, I believe sincerely that Manchester United would have become the first British club to carry off the European Cup—and that we might well have retained it for two or three seasons. We shall never know, of course, whether I would have been proved right in this belief, but in my view the team of season 1957–58 was approaching its peak—and it was already being labelled a great side.

But you have to face reality, and the reality of the situation in the spring of 1958 was that United needed time . . . time to mould another team. Even though we had so much young talent, you cannot lose a dozen or so players at a stroke and carry on as if nothing had happened.

So it took 10 more years before United finally achieved that ambition in Europe and, in the process, I built yet another team, took it apart, and built again.

THE MANY moods of Matt Busby . . . relaxed and smiling; scanning the skyline as he sits between Jimmy Murphy and Mark Jones; making a point to physiotherapist Ted Dalton; shading his eyes from the sun; and at times looking positively pensive, as he grapples with the immediate problems of Soccer.

CA

NDID CAMERA

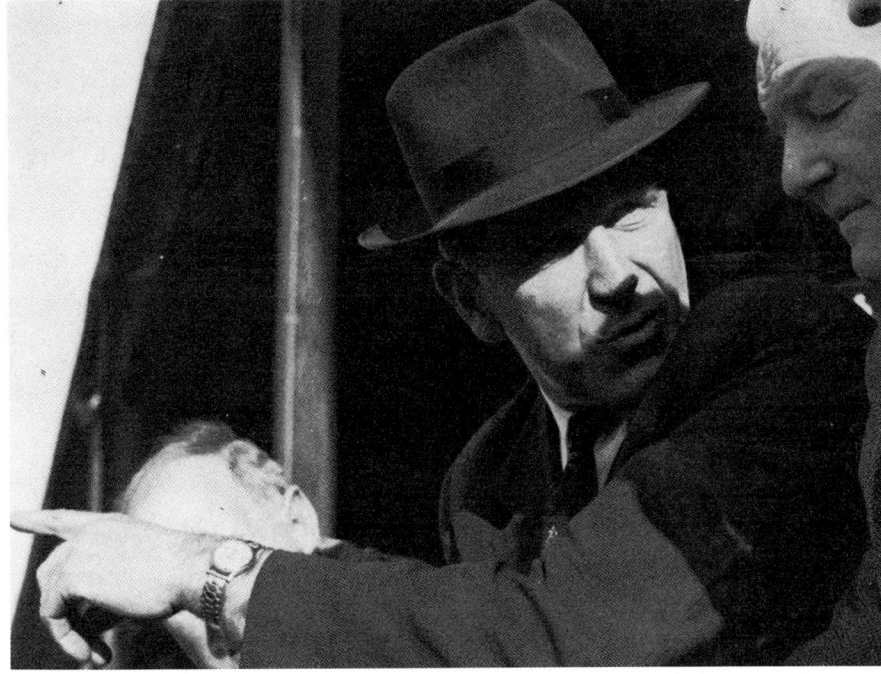

PARTY
GAMES

LEFT : Party time for the youngsters, as they meet Matt Busby ; right, a waiting game, as the ladies prepare to welcome United home from the Cup in 1957.

FOOTBALL can be fun . . . especially when you've won. Left, United fans en route to the 1948 F.A. Cup final; top left, the victors' banquet. Far left, Frank Swift 'sinks' a bottle, as Sandy Busby and Don Gibson—United men both—enjoy a spot of fraternising with a City star. Top picture, United's civic reception at Stretford in May, 1957; above (left), Shay Brennan and Paddy Crerand give Nobby Stiles a cloth-cap fitting and (above right, and right), cake-cutting time, with Johnny Carey helping Matt Busby do the honours in Hollywood

45

STEPPING out in style—left to right: Matt Busby, Jackie Balmer, Jim Harley, Willie Fagan and Dick Kemp, all of whom wore the colours of Liverpool.

More Reflections from the past

MORE Soccer stars in uniform ... and they include Andy Beattie (fourth man in on the back row), with Wilf Copping (to the left of Matt Busby) and Don Welsh and Maurice Edelston (to the right) on the front row.

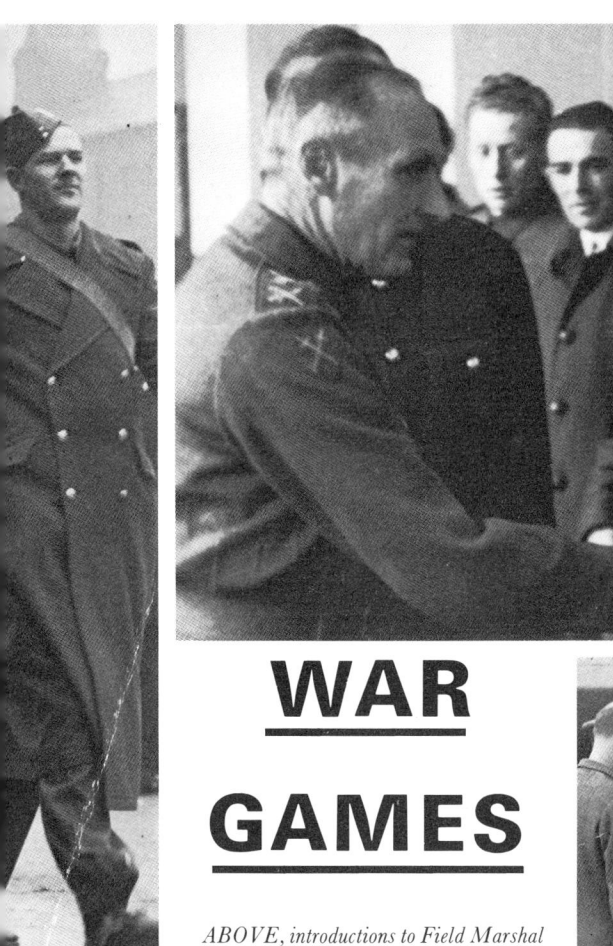

WAR GAMES

ABOVE, introductions to Field Marshal Montgomery; right, another pre-match chat as Matt Busby leads a British Army side; below, a Services team which included Matt Busby, Neil Franklin, George Smith, George Hardwick, Maurice Edelston, Tommy Lawton, Bert Williams, Bert Sproston and Stan Mortensen.

SOCCER stars in uniform (below), and in case you're trying to puzzle out their identities, the players (from left to right) on the back row are Joe Mercer, Frank Soo, Maurice Edelston, and on the front row Frank Swift, Stanley Matthews and Matt Busby. Left: Matt Busby with an international who starred for England in another sport . . . C. B. Holmes, the noted sprinter.

THE INTERNATIONAL SET

TWO WEMBLEY shots, with Matt Busby skippering Scotland against England in a wartime international (above), as 'keeper Jerry Dawson watches the defensive action; and (top right) another picture of Dawson, making a save. The game was staged to boost Mrs. Churchill's Aid to Russia fund, in 1942.

HOME and away (right), as Matt Busby leads out the
Scotland team against England at Hampden Park and, along
with Frank Swift, lines up for a match with the Army side, as
the scene switches to Rome in May, 1945. The end of the war
was in sight, and within a short time Matt Busby was to take on
a new job—as manager of Manchester United.

49

FAR-AWAY PLACES

SOCCER business can take you around the world, and Matt Busby has travelled widely. Above, boarding the plane for Dubrovnik, Yugoslavia; left, taking it easy after a game in Poland against Gornik. Top right, 'down under' . . . and a friendly encounter with a Maori warrior in New Zealand; centre right, sampling the sunshine in the George Cross island of Malta; and right, in the sheriff's office in Detroit, Michigan, U.S.A.

STRANGE-SOUNDING NAMES

51

FAR-AWAY PLACES

and some FAMOUS FACES

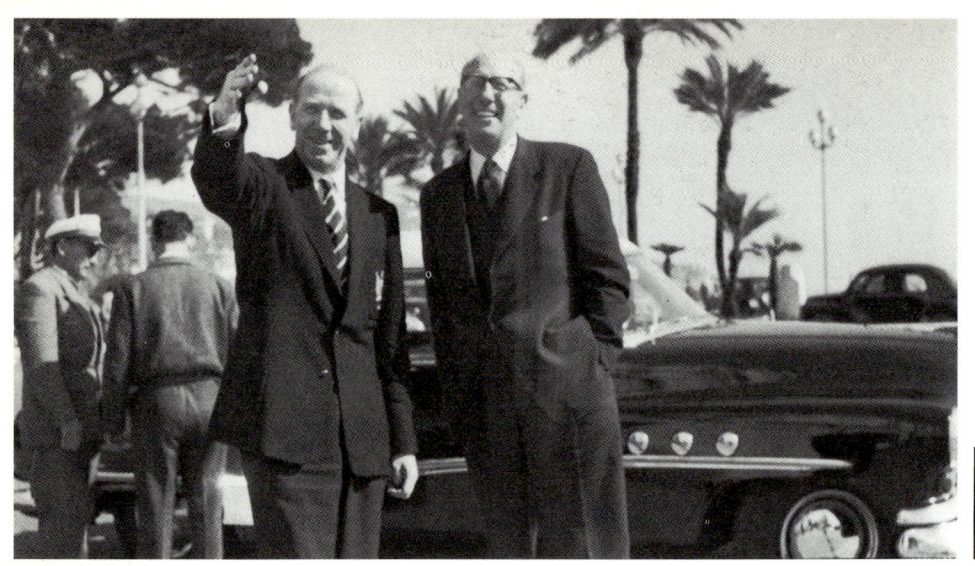

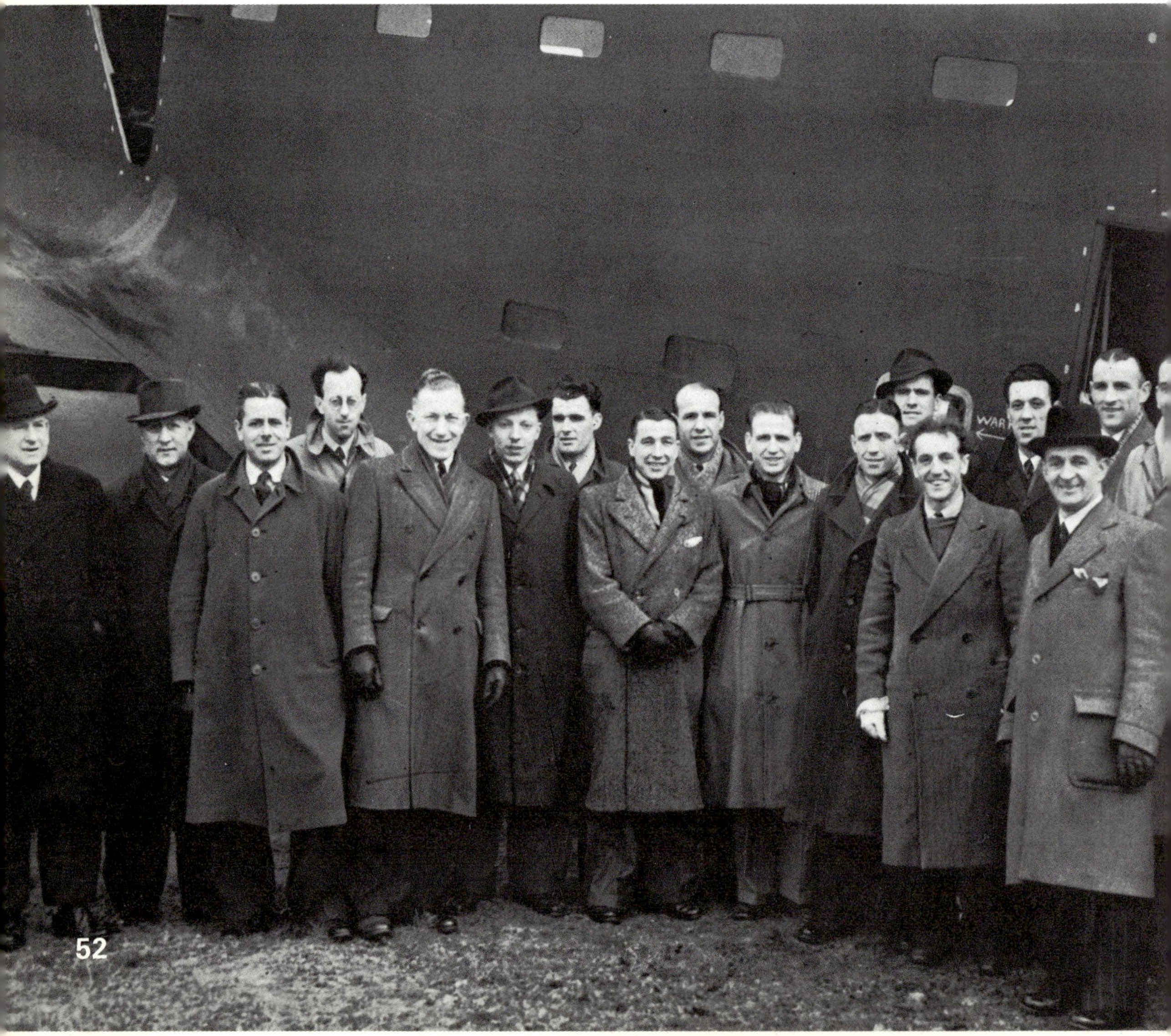

FAR LEFT, Matt Busby enjoys the sunshine in the south of France—but he's on football business, for he's there to watch a European Cup quarter-final between Nice and Real Madrid (whom United met in the semi-finals). With him is sportswriter Archie Ledbrooke, who lost his life as a result of the Munich air crash in 1958. Bottom left, Manchester United's team of the late 1940's takes to the air, bound for Celle, and a game in Germany.

THE first trip United made to the United States, and the top picture shows them with Bing Crosby in Hollywood, on the set of 'Road to Bali'. Above, another famous film face—the man in the centre of the picture is comedian Jerry Lewis. And left, smiles all round again, as United's players relax by the pool.

53

JUST THE TICKET?—T-H-I-S IS WHAT IT MEANS, WHEN YOU GET TO WEMBLEY!

OVER THE years since 1945, Manchester United have become familiar with Wembley, as they have appeared there in the European Cup final, F.A. Cup finals and Charity Shield matches. There was 1948, 1957, 1958, 1963, 1968 during Matt Busby's reign as manager, and the picture below shows what it means, when the fans start clamouring for those precious tickets. Here Matt Busby and secretary Walter Crickmer handle just some of the 'traffic' which passed through Old Trafford before the 1957 final . . . in the shape of numerous applications for 'just one ticket' for Wembley.

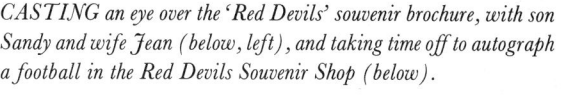

THE Manchester United Soccer family (above) on arrival in New York. Back row (left to right): Director Alan Gibson, Jack Crompton, Bill Foulkes, Alex Dawson, Joe Carolan, Harry Gregg, Frank Haydock, Albert Scanlon, Matt Busby. Front row: chairman Harold Hardman, Tom Heron, Nobby Lawton, Johnny Giles, Mark Pearson, Shay Brennan, Albert Quixall, Ronnie Cope.

CASTING an eye over the 'Red Devils' souvenir brochure, with son Sandy and wife Jean (below, left), and taking time off to autograph a football in the Red Devils Souvenir Shop (below).

TWENTY YEARS on . . . Harry Gregg is back with Manchester United, after spells in management at Shrewsbury, Swansea and Crewe. Back to the club where, as a goalkeeper, he achieved fame . . . and now he's the man responsible for putting United's goalkeeper of the present, Gary Bailey, through his paces. Under Gregg, Bailey has developed from an unknown into an England Under-21 player.

AND 20

YEARS ON

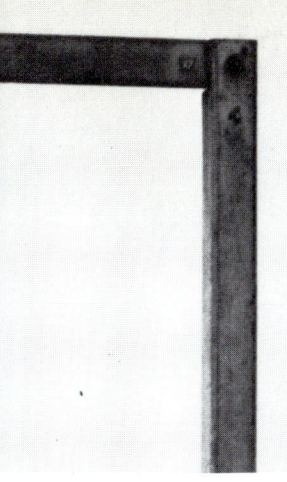

THE INTRODUCTION
OF A
NEW BOY

THIS was the first day at Manchester United for goalkeeper Harry Gregg (left) away back in December, 1957, after he had been signed from Doncaster Rovers for a then world-record transfer fee of £23,500. Gregg was already a Northern Ireland international, and in the 1958 World Cup in Sweden he topped the poll and was voted the world's No. 1 'keeper. On that first day of training with United, the new boy met the players who were to become his team-mates, and here Gregg (pictured also inset) is being tested out by Duncan Edwards.

THESE pictures form a part of United's history; they capture the smiles and tears of a bygone era. On the left, walking in the sunshine, are Johnny Berry, Liam Whelan, Dennis Viollet, Mark Jones, Tommy Taylor and David Pegg. Top left, Roger Byrne and Harry Gregg in action against Ipswich at Old Trafford—a game United won 2–0. In the team that day, also, were Duncan Edwards, Bill Foulkes and Eddie Colman. It was 12 days before Munich . . .

Now look at the picture above—a tragically historic one, for it shows the United line-up minutes before the start of the European Cup-tie against Red Star in Belgrade. From left to right: Duncan Edwards, Eddie Colman, Mark Jones, Kenny Morgans, Bobby

SUNSHINE . . .
AND SHADOWS

Charlton, Dennis Viollet, Tommy Taylor, Bill Foulkes, Harry Gregg, Albert Scanlon and Roger Byrne. A matter of hours after the final whistle, the world reeled as the shock news broke about Munich. And United's team had been decimated.

MUNICH

BLACK DAY for Manchester United . . . February 6, 1958. It was an air disaster which destroyed a team and it became known by a single word . . . Munich. Inset above (left to right), United men who lost their lives: Walter Crickmer, Tom Curry, Bert Whalley, Tommy Taylor, David Pegg, Geoff. Bent, Eddie Colman, Roger Byrne, Mark Jones, Duncan Edwards, Liam Whelan. And this was the scene on the snowswept airstrip as a United survivor, Harry Gregg, surveys the havoc.

ELIZABETHAN CLASS
RMA LORD BURGHLEY

TWO MEN WHO SURVIVED . . .

CLOSE-UP of the stricken aircraft . . . and a feeling of relief for two of the Manchester United men who survived. Harry Gregg and Bill Foulkes brave the cold to retrace their steps through slush and snow to the airstrip at Munich, where so many of their team-mates lost their lives or were injured so badly that they never played again.

MUNICH

FLAMES leap skywards (below, right), torn and jagged metal (right) presents another stark piece of evidence as to the carnage caused by the Munich air crash, as rescue workers do their best to get to grips with a nightmare situation.

I HEARD A VOICE SAYING . . . 'THIS ONE—HE IS DEAD'

TWO DECADES and more later, I can still vividly recall some of the events of the Munich air disaster, which happened on 6 February 1958—the blackest day in the history of Manchester United and, indeed, of British football. It was a tragedy which, for a brief while, brought me to a stage of such despair that I cared not whether I lived or died and, even when I was recovering, I remained so overwhelmed by grief that it was in my mind to sever my ties with football.

The details of the crash need no elaboration. It is sufficient to say that on 6 February, on an airstrip at Munich, Manchester United lost a great team and I lost players, officials and Pressmen whom I had counted as friends. My own injuries were such that, after the crash, my first memory of consciousness centres around a room in the hospital and I was vaguely aware of lying on a trolley while all around me there seemed to be other trolleys with people in a similar situation.

For a split second I heard a voice saying: 'This one'—and I even recall the name mentioned—'he is dead.' The reference was to Frank Swift, one-time Manchester City and England goalkeeper turned sportswriter, and a jovial companion on many a footballing occasion.

I remember hearing another voice—I think it was that of Professor Georg Maurer—giving the person who had spoken hell for mentioning the word 'dead' . . . then I must have drifted away into a state of limbo, because not until several days later did I return to the land of the living, and even then my physical state was so feeble that death could still have been touching me.

When my mind did begin to take things in, I knew things had been bad. But because the facts were kept

from me for a while after that, I had no way of knowing the details of the losses football—yes, and the newspapers—had suffered. One day, I recall, someone came into the room and said something to the effect that many people were dead.

Eventually my wife, Jean, was allowed to see me and I learned the true state of affairs. I would mention a name, and she would nod or shake her head. Those actions told me who still lived and who had died.

If I had begun to feel slightly more like a human being again, that news was a setback—I found it too terrible to contemplate, and I was ready to give up, not really caring whether I lived or died. When I thought of football, I told myself there was no way I could resume my own career in the game. Too much had happened for me to want to be a part of it again.

Through all the ordeals of mind and body which I suffered, it seemed there was no way ahead for me, and when it was discovered that I had a lung puncture, once more I was prepared for death. I had lain there with tubes down my throat, I had endured pain, I had seen people doing things to my legs and

MUNICH

feet, and when they told me about the lung, I whispered to myself: 'This must be the end . . .'

It was Jean, at my side through all the trials I suffered, who first planted in my brain the germ of the will to survive—and to carry on.

Never for an instant did she betray any of the doubts and agonies she must have been enduring, and one day she murmured softly to me a dozen words or so which, I am now thankful to say, stuck in my mind. 'Matt,' she said, 'I am sure those boys who are gone would want you to carry on.'

My first inclination was to dismiss those words . . . but they would not go away. And as I lay there—I spent the best part of three months in the hospital— the idea began to take root that I might, after all, return to gather up the reins again at Manchester United. It was a gradual process, just as my recovery was gradual, and on my last day Professor Maurer

GERMAN rescue workers toil in and around the shattered plane . . . but life goes on all around, and (above left) another aircraft takes to the sky over Munich as the grim work on the ground continues.

came to me and offered this advice: 'Now go and get some good air into your lungs . . . go to Interlaken or the Black Forest.'

I was hobbling around on two sticks, I didn't feel as if I wanted to talk to people or even face them. But the world was still revolving outside that hospital and Professor Maurer—the man who had done most to bring me back from the brink of the grave—had done all he could for my physical welfare. So I took his advice and went to Interlaken for six weeks.

Eventually, I had to face the decision to return to Manchester—and that meant Old Trafford. It was a haunting, nightmare experience, but if I were to act upon Jean's words it had to be done. By then Manchester United—patched up with new faces in the side—had reached the final of the F.A. Cup, and I visited the players and Jimmy Murphy at their Blackpool training headquarters.

I was advised not to go to Wembley, but I did. However it was Jimmy—and rightly so, even had I been fit—who led the team out for the pre-match presentations.

So I returned to football, although it took me the best part of two years to steel myself to fly again. And that was another ordeal. For two years after the crash, whenever United played abroad they went by boat or train. But this state of affairs could not be allowed to continue for ever—it wasn't being fair to the club or the players. So, without telling anyone, I decided to put myself to the test, and—with the late chairman Louis Edwards, who had been brought on to the board after the crash—I boarded an aircraft at Ringway, bound for Rotterdam.

It was little more than an hour's flight, but I found that even a few stiff brandies didn't quell the feeling of terror which churned my insides. And it was no easier on the return flight. However, I made it, and that was the end of another trial for me.

I think here is a good place to talk about all the

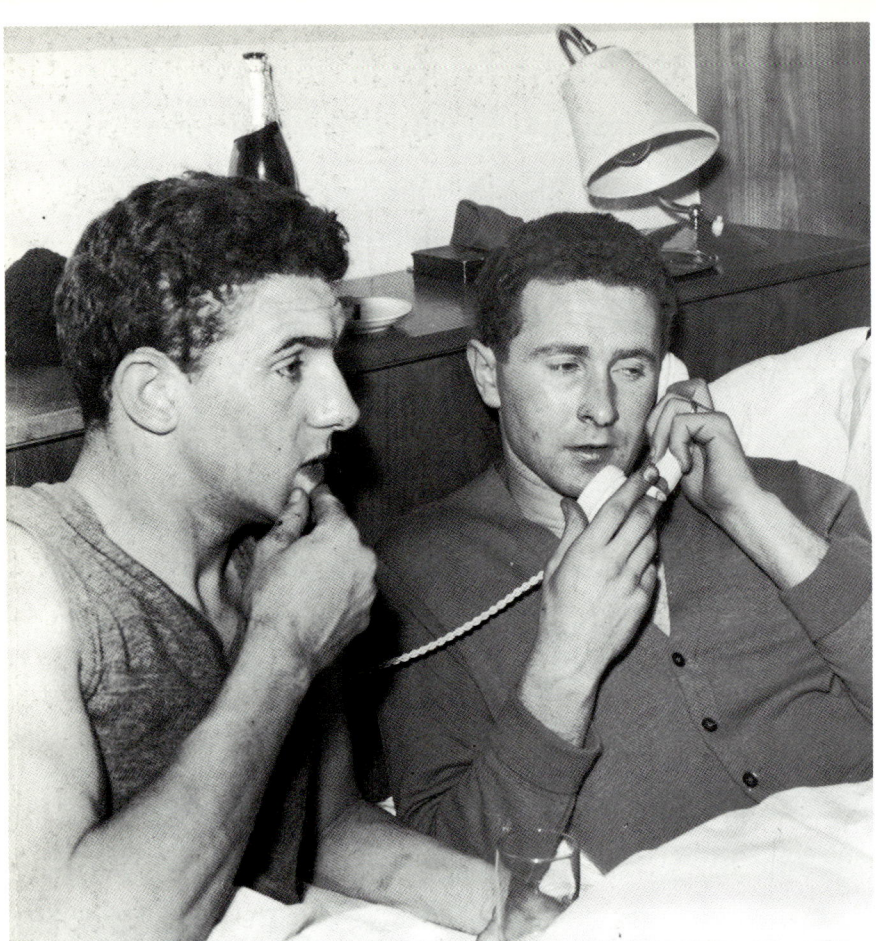

sentiment which swept the country after Munich like a huge wave. I must admit that for a long time I remained too upset even to think about it, but I have since come to recognise that, eventually, there were people who felt Manchester United had had too much of a good thing.

I can speak only for myself, but I can honestly say that I never got caught up in that gigantic wave of sentiment, and that I never felt the club was cashing in on it. Once I had taken charge at Old Trafford again, I had other things on my mind—like building a team again. For while United had gone to Wembley in the spring of 1958, and while we had finished as First Division runners-up 12 months after that, I realised that we were in a false position. A lot of work remained to be done before we could claim we had achieved our goal.

People have been kind enough to say that I was as good at public relations as I was at managing a football team—some have even suggested that I was a better P.R.O. than I was a manager. All I can say is

MUNICH

The sentiment which swept the country . . .

that I never set out to be a public-relations man . . . my mission was to build a team. But I always recognised that others—the Press, for instance—were a part of the game and entitled to consideration.

So I tried to co-operate with everyone as far as possible, without disclosing all the club's business. There were times when the newspapers wanted to know things, and if I could help, I did. There were occasions, also, where I felt I had to protect the

THE MAN whose skills helped Matt Busby to live (right) . . . surgeon Professor Georg Maurer takes a bow at Old Trafford before United go out to play, with the memory of Munich behind them and their manager back in harness. And above, a greeting from Mrs. Maurer for Harry Gregg, as she pins a Munich 'angel of mercy' badge upon his jersey.

MUNICH

club—but if someone pinned me down with a direct question, I didn't duck the issue. I tried not to mislead, and I didn't tell lies.

After Munich, I became obsessed with restoring Manchester United to the pinnacle, and, when I felt the occasion warranted, I sought help from others, such as Santiago Bernabeu, the president of Real Madrid. Once, in my endeavours to keep the name of United before the public, I flew to Madrid and asked Senor Bernabeu if Real would play us in a showgame at Old Trafford.

I was completely honest with him, as I said: 'We have no money . . . and I know that Real Madrid can command huge fees for playing exhibition matches abroad. If you say "No", I shall understand.' Real's president pondered a moment, then motioned to the club secretary, saying: 'We shall play—for expenses only.' And they did.

That incident happened about two years after Munich, at a time when we were still struggling to get back on our feet, and I appreciated Real's gesture, just as I appreciated the help of many other people who had my club's interests at heart.

Let me also add that in talking about the Munich disaster, I have done so not with any idea of making myself look a saint or a hero, nor with the thought of any personal glory. Munich happened—and many times I have wished that it hadn't been so. It was woven inextricably into my career as manager of Manchester United. So it could not be ignored, and I have told it just as it was.

1958

THE CHANGING FACES AT OLD TRAFFORD

TIMES and faces change as years go by, and these pictures show how the changes have been rung at Old Trafford through the years. The top picture features the first-team squad after Munich, in 1958; then comes the era of the early 1960's, as United carried off the F.A. Cup at Wembley in 1963. It was still Matt Busby's team then. But 14 years on, when United claimed the trophy again, Tommy Docherty was the team boss and SIR Matt Busby was a director of United.

THE 1980'S

THE top picture shows United's playing squad during the 1970's, in the days when Frank O'Farrell was the manager at Old Trafford. And above, Dave Sexton is the team boss as Manchester United meet the challenge of the 1980s.

FACE TO FACE WITH THE FANS —AND THE FUTURE

THE MOMENT when the survivors of the Munich disaster have to face the fans—and the future—again at Old Trafford. This was United's first game since the air crash . . . an F.A. Cup-tie against Sheffield Wednesday. Leading out the team is Bill Foulkes; behind him comes Alex Dawson, then Harry Gregg and Colin Webster. It's a makeshift side, composed of experience and newcomers . . . but United, given an almost hysterical welcome from their fans, swept Wednesday off the Wembley trail.

UNITED ARISE FROM THE ASHES OF MUNICH

LIKE the phoenix, Manchester United arose from the ashes . . . in their case, the ashes of Munich. Above, the new-look playing staff at Old Trafford, as Jimmy Murphy took charge in the absence of Matt Busby. Ranged alongside him on the front row are chief scout Joe Armstrong, Bill Inglis and (extreme right) Jack Crompton. Behind, the 22 players who comprised the professional staff.

LEFT, the first-team squad, reading from left to right (back row): Bobby Harrop, Ian Greaves, Freddie Goodwin, Harry Gregg, Stan Crowther (signed from Aston Villa), Ronnie Cope, Shay Brennan; and (front row) Jack Crompton, Alex Dawson, Mark Pearson, Bill Foulkes, Bobby Charlton, Ernie Taylor (signed from Blackpool), Colin Webster and Bill Inglis.

UNITED'S European Cup line-up (above) for the semi-final against A.C. Milan in Italy, in 1958. Left to right: Foulkes, Pearson, Gregg, Webster, Viollet, Morgans, Greaves, Goodwin, Cope, Taylor, Crowther. Top right, Gregg in action.

GLAD to be alive! Right, Bobby Charlton, Harry Gregg and Dennis Viollet meet sports writer Frank Taylor, another Munich survivor, while Albert Quixall—a post-Munich record signing by United, at £45,000—joins in the greeting.

RETURN to Munich for Matt Busby (far right)—and this time it's a happy occasion, as he signs the distinguished-visitors' book.

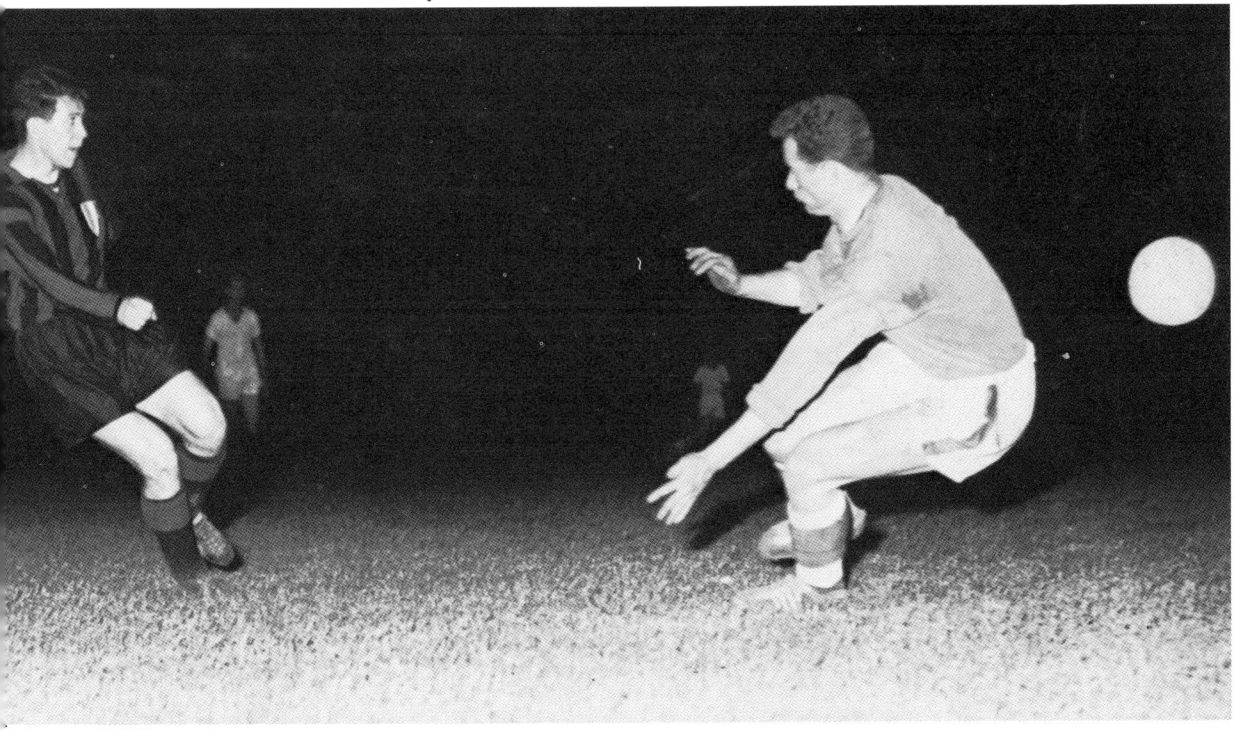

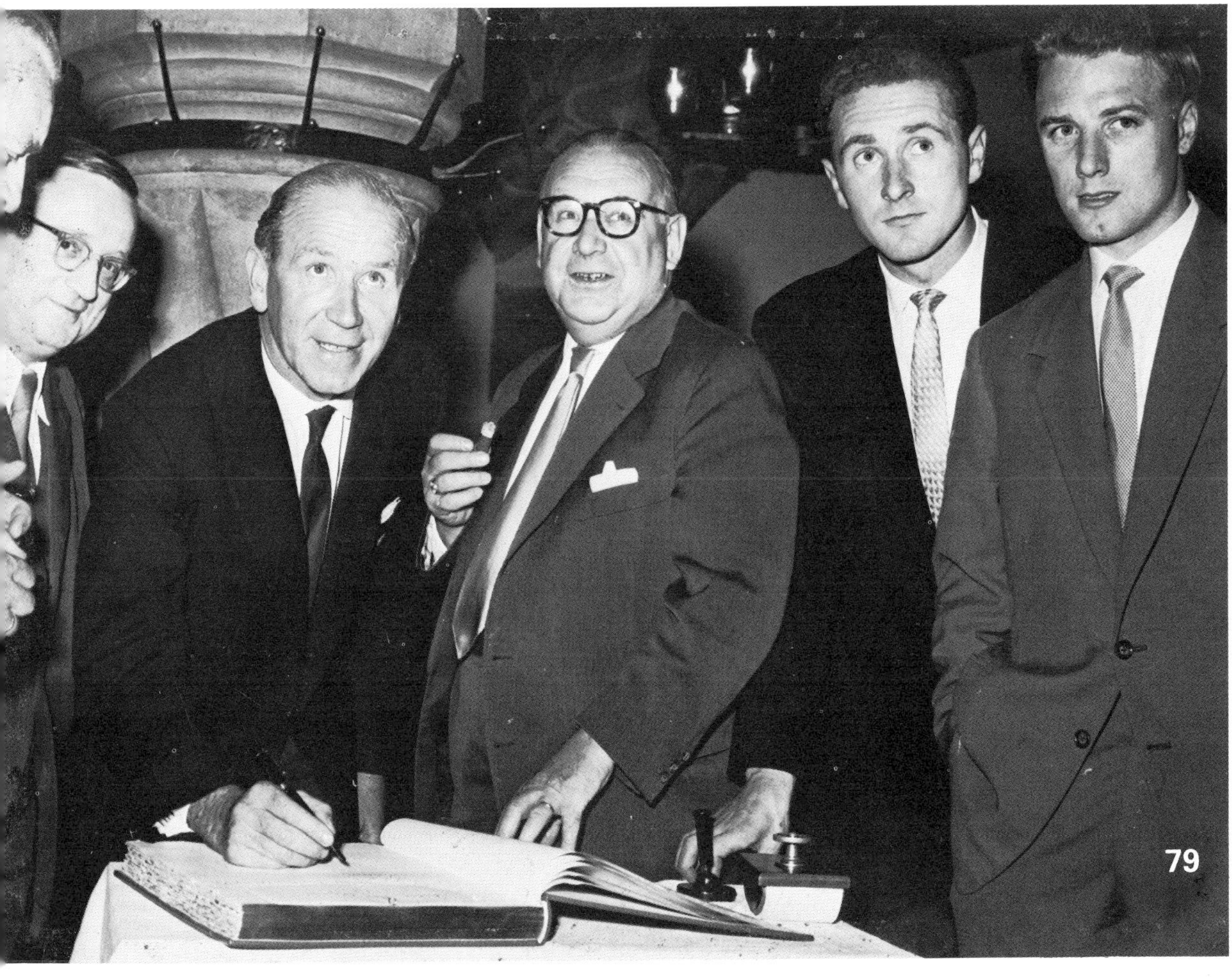

HAIL . . .
AND
FAREWELL

MATT BUSBY *leaves the Rechts der Isar hospital in 1958 (above), and says farewell to Professor Maurer, whose skills helped him to recover after the air crash at Munich. Left, a warm welcome from Matt Busby for Albert Quixall, who cost a record, £45,000 transfer fee when United signed him from Sheffield Wednesday.*

THE LAST OF THE BUSBY BABES

IN FULL FLIGHT . . . Sammy McIlroy, the last of the original Busby Babes. Matt Busby signed him as a youngster from Belfast, and McIlroy has served under five managers at Old Trafford . . . Matt Busby, Wilf McGuinness, Frank O'Farrell, Tommy Docherty and Dave Sexton. What price now, a player who cost Manchester United nothing?

ON THE WAY TO
W-E-M-B-L-E-Y

MANCHESTER UNITED regrouped, recruited new players . . . and, despite the body-blow of Munich, battled on to reach the final of the F.A. Cup in 1958. Munich survivors like Harry Gregg, Bill Foulkes, Bobby Charlton and Dennis Viollet were the backbone of the team; newcomers like Ernie Taylor and Stan Crowther added experience; and players such as Ian Greaves, Freddie Goodwin, Ronnie Cope, Alex Dawson and Colin Webster—all drafted in from the reserves—also made their mark.

THIS WAS the action in the 1958 F.A. Cup semi-final tussles with Fulham. Top picture: Jimmy Hill beats Harry Gregg and Bill Foulkes to score Fulham's second goal and force a replay; centre picture: goalmouth action again, but United men Ronnie Cope and Bill Foulkes see Harry Gregg tip the ball safely over the bar. Above, a youthful-looking Bobby Charlton watches Gregg make a finger-tip save from Johnny Haynes; and left, action from the Highbury replay . . . which United won, 5–3.

UNITED'S squad in season 1962–63: Denis Law, Shay Brennan, Bill Foulkes, Ted Dalton (physiotherapist), Maurice Setters, David Gaskell, Harry Gregg, Paddy Crerand, Jack Crompton (trainer), Tony Dunne, Albert Quixall, Noell Cantwell, David Herd, Nobby Stiles, Johnny Giles, Bobby Charlton.

CENTRE pictures: Matt Busby leads the 1963 F.A. Cup-final team out at Wembley, and Denis Law meets the Duke of Edinburgh. The two pictures above show Leicester

'keeper Gordon Banks snatching the ball to safety after a Law effort had hit a post, and leaping desperately, but in vain, to prevent a goal by Law.

OUT AT WEMBLEY . . .

AND THE ACTION

GOALS from David Herd (above and left), as the United striker hits home No. 2 and No. 3, to leave Banks helpless.

ONE OF the most harassing periods of my managerial career was in season 1962–63, when Manchester United were struggling to stay in the First Division, despite the acquisition of players such as Paddy Crerand, Denis Law and Albert Quixall. It was not that I ever felt that I had a bad team, nor was there ever any suggestion that my job was at stake, but it was a worrying time.

I knew the team needed a breathing space, to give the players the chance to knit together as a unit. I also felt that luck was against me, and I felt sick at heart as I saw results going against us. I remember a match at Filbert Street when Law scored a hat-trick . . . and Leicester City still beat us, 4–3. After the game I told the players confidently: 'If we keep on playing like this, we *must* get results' . . . but that didn't alter the fact that we were struggling.

One Sunday morning I drove down to Old Trafford, and was surprised when chairman Harold Hardman walked in. We had had another bad result on the Saturday, and I wondered what the chairman's presence meant, although it never occurred to me for a moment that my job was at risk.

It wasn't—but what the chairman had to say to me was still somewhat unexpected, for he was a man who, usually, offered neither criticism nor praise. If things were going well, he wasn't fulsome, and you simply carried on doing your job; and up to that season, I had never really had any cause for worry about United's League position.

The chairman wasted no time in preliminaries. He said: 'Look, Matt, I've come down here especially, and for one reason only—to tell you that you must not worry about this situation.' Coming from him, those words really meant something, and I felt his gesture was one of the greatest things that had happened to me in football.

Even while we were making progress in the F.A. Cup, we were not getting results in the League, and the time came when we had to play Manchester City at Maine Road towards the end of the season. We desperately needed two points. We scored the only goal of the game, from a penalty. And, in the final analysis, we stayed in the First Division. We also went to Wembley and beat Leicester City to carry off the F.A. Cup.

Nobody needs to remind me that during the season there were criticisms of the team, and there were times when not all the players at Old Trafford were happy. The criticisms were inevitable, considering

RIGHT, the moment that United know the F.A. Cup is coming their way, as striker David Herd beats Leicester 'keeper Gordon Banks and slots the ball into the net for goal No. 2 in the 1963 final at Wembley.

A HARD TIME IN THE LEAGUE . . . SUCCESS IN THE F.A. CUP

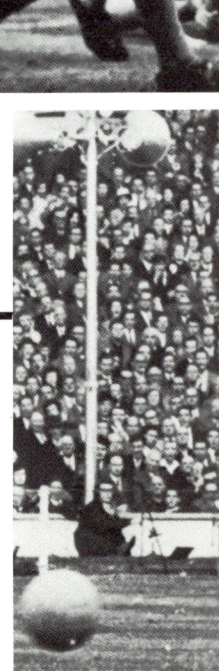

HERE'S a close-up of the right-footer from David Herd that brought goal No. 3—and again Banks is stranded, as the United striker hammers the ball into the net. No doubt about it now . . . United are in control, and all set to carry off the F.A. Cup.

that a great deal of money had been spent in trying to rebuild the side . . . £56,000 for Paddy Crerand, £45,000 for Albert Quixall, £115,000 for Denis Law, £40,000 for David Herd, and around £30,000 apiece for Maurice Setters and Noel Cantwell.

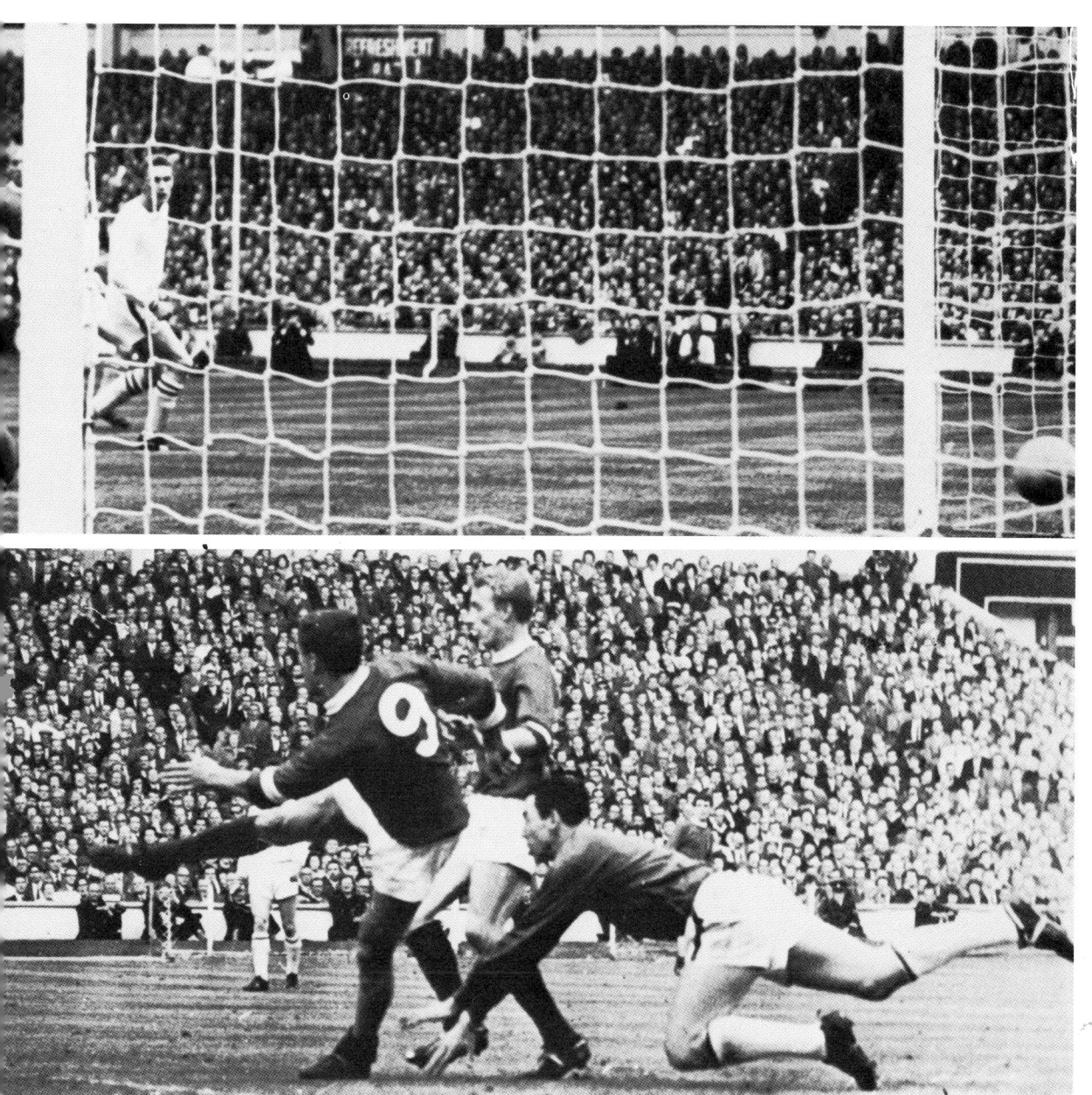

I think I can claim that the critics came round, in the end. Those who had called Paddy Crerand slow as a carthorse began to appreciate the artistry of a player who could make precision passes and dictate the pattern of the game. It was no idle statement that when Crerand was on song, so were United.

Albert Quixall had been the 'golden boy' at Sheffield Wednesday, and at the time I signed him he cost a record fee. He was a dainty player, with natural skills, and he was a creative player, like Crerand. I

UP for the Cup . . . and the Queen presents the glittering trophy to United skipper Noel Cantwell, after the 1963 final victory over Leicester City at Wembley.

WHY GILES WAS SOLD TO LEEDS

THE waiting game at Old Trafford was not for Johnny Giles (above, left) . . . so Don Revie was able to snap up a player who became Leeds United's midfield general. Matt Busby didn't want to lose Giles, but patience wasn't the name of the game.

was trying to give Manchester United the kind of flair for which they had been famous, and I believe Quixall, who did a good job for us, justified the fee.

However, even when we had reached the final of the F.A. Cup, there were problems. Harry Gregg had been injured, so David Gaskell had taken over in goal, and when Harry was fit again, I still gave David a vote of confidence. We had managed to win some matches, and I felt the obvious thing was to keep a settled side.

When it came to naming the team for the final, I faced one or two more tricky decisions. In the end, this was the line-up: Gaskell; Dunne, Cantwell; Crerand, Foulkes, Setters; Giles, Quixall, Herd, Law, Charlton.

Which meant that little Nobby Stiles was unhappy at having been left out, while his brother-in-law, Johnny Giles, had a place on the right wing, although I knew he preferred to play at inside-forward. Nobby was annoyed that he hadn't been chosen, and he came to see me; but he didn't press for a transfer, and I was thankful for that. He was Manchester United through and through, and I felt that while he had to be disappointed then, there would be other great occasions for him in the future. And indeed there were.

Johnny Giles presented problems because he had a great deal of skill, but he still hadn't reached a stage where he could regard himself as a regular. He was young enough to have time on his side, and I felt he would develop into a great player. I tried to explain my point of view to Johnny, and I hoped he would be patient.

However, Johnny clearly felt that his career was not progressing as quickly as he would like, and eventually we agreed that a transfer was the solution. When Don Revie stepped in to offer £40,000, I told him exactly why Johnny was being allowed to go, and after his move to Leeds he became one of the finest midfield players in English League football.

People have asked me more than once if Johnny Giles wasn't one of my mistakes. My answer remains the same: given the situation as it was, and if it were to be repeated, I would still take the same decision. Reluctantly, of course . . . and I wouldn't be honest if I didn't admit that there were times, after Johnny had left Old Trafford, when I wished he had stayed.

At least Johnny helped Manchester United to win the F.A. Cup in season 1962–63, so he wound up with a medal to show for his days at Old Trafford, and with David Herd scoring two goals and Denis Law getting one, the 3–1 victory over Leicester City enabled us to smile again after the disappointments of the League campaign.

READY for the champagne celebrations . . . left to right: David Gaskell, Tony Dunne, Bobby Charlton, Pat Crerand, Noel Cantwell, Albert Quixall, David Herd, Johnny Giles and Maurice Setters after victory over Leicester in the 1963 F.A. Cup final.

IF the cap fits . . . only in this case, it's not the cap, but the F.A. Cup, and Denis Law is the man in the middle between David Herd and Maurice Setters. On the right, a youthful-looking Bobby Charlton seems a bit pensive, as if he's still trying to take in the fact that United have won.

STAR TREK

BY THE early 1960s, I was beginning to see signs of a new Manchester United side emerging, but I knew in my heart that it was not quite championship material. The team had been moulded largely as a result of improvisation as we rebuilt after Munich, and it was capable of winning half a dozen key matches and bringing the F.A. Cup to Old Trafford, as happened in 1963.

However, I felt strongly that one man could supply the essential ingredient for sustained success: Denis Law.

The story of my quest for Law still reads like Soccer fiction, but it is fact. It began after we had lost an F.A. Cup semi-final against Tottenham Hotspur at Hillsborough, and I had made up my mind that Denis must be my target. So I went to London, where I had arranged to meet the manager of Law's club, Torino.

I went armed with the knowledge that reports from Italy suggested Denis was not of a mind to stay there, and Torino's manager confirmed this for me. It was agreed that if there were any developments, I would be kept posted, and in due course a second meeting was arranged, this time in Amsterdam with another official of Torino.

Amsterdam was convenient because Real Madrid were playing Benfica in the European Cup final there, and I wanted to see the match. United's chairman at the time, Mr. Harold Hardman, travelled with me.

There had been talk that Juventus would like to sign Denis, but I felt that with Juventus and Torino being such great rivals in the same city, Manchester United must have the edge not only with the player, but with Torino.

We also expected to get down to discussions with the Italian representative at once, but on our arrival at our hotel found a message to say that, because of other business, the meeting must be postponed to another date.

THE picture that signalled the end of Matt Busby's Star Trek (above) . . . Denis Law, flanked by Gigi Peronace, Jimmy Murphy and his new boss, signs the forms that make him a Manchester United player, at a cost of £115,000. And here, too, is Law as the fans often saw him . . . leaping like a salmon to head the ball, and arms upraised as he hails the scoring of a goal.

I cannot say I was happy about that turn of events, but there was nothing Mr. Hardman or I could do except stay over for the final and hope that contact would be renewed. I suggested to the chairman that we should go out for a meal, and asked the hall porter if he could recommend a nice restaurant. He gave me two names and—since I had no knowledge of either—I said to Mr. Hardman: 'Come on . . . we'll go to this one.'

It was a beautiful restaurant, and we were seated at a table enjoying our meal when I just happened to look up as some people came past. I was staggered to see that it was the Italian official whom we had been due to meet for talks about Denis Law . . . and he was

escorting a gorgeous blonde. So that was obviously the 'business' which had taken precedence over football-transfer talk.

As it happened, I knew the official, and when he saw me he scarcely knew which way to look—especially when, feeling very put out by what I considered to be his discourteous treatment of us, I asked him point-blank: 'What kind of game are you playing?'

STAR TREK

And finally, I lost my temper. . .

Immediately, he apologised and agreed to meet us at 11 o'clock the next morning.

Next day, no mention was made of the previous evening, and we got down to discussing the business which had taken us to Amsterdam. I started by suggesting that Manchester United should sign Denis Law and that we should pay Torino £90,000 for the privilege. The Torino official thought that figure too low, and although we stepped up our bid more than once, he kept on asking for more. Our meeting ended without anything conclusive being agreed.

I still felt that Denis would become a Manchester United player, but I couldn't spend every waking minute chasing Torino to get a 'Yes' out of them. So I sat tight, and hoped for the best. When a phone call came, it was Gigi Peronace saying that Torino would like to meet me again, this time in Lausanne. So I packed my bags once more.

Gigi and a representative of Torino were waiting for me, and I thought, 'This time I'm going to get my man.' Wrong again—we still couldn't finalise a fee which suited both clubs. So home I went.

I travelled with the team for a short break in Majorca, and—having been warned to expect another call—waited in the hotel most of the day. Just as I was about to give it up, Gigi Peronace rang through and asked if I would fly from Majorca to a rendezvous in Turin. At last, it seemed, I was getting to the heart of the matter.

Chairman Harold Hardman, director Louis Edwards and myself boarded a plane for Italy, met directors of Torino . . . and, it seemed, had come up against a brick wall yet again. All they appeared to be interest in was telling us how much *Juventus* were prepared to pay them, to get Denis Law.

To me, it had become a long-running serial in which Manchester United were being given the runaround, and I finally lost my temper. I told them bluntly that they had dragged us to Italy on a wild-goose chase.

We had flown to Turin under the firm impression

DENIS: A LAW UNTO HIMSELF

THE MERCURIAL Denis Law, pictured once more in familiar on-field situations. Left, he's wearing the colours of Manchester City and it's a derby game against Manchester United . . . which means the opposing 'keeper is Harry Gregg; below left, having words with the referee; and below, wearing the colours of Manchester United and making his presence felt in the opposition's goalmouth.

I told my chairman: 'Let's get to hell out of here'

that this time, the way was clear for us to sign the player . . . and there we were, being put through the wringer again. My chairman was an elderly man, and I felt he had been subjected to enough. 'Come on, Mr. Hardman,' I said to him, 'let's get to hell out of here.'

The following morning we were all set to turn our backs on sunny Italy when I received a call from the chairman of Juventus, Signor Agnelli, asking to see me. So I postponed my departure to listen to what *he* had to say. Signor Agnelli came straight to the point. 'We want to clear the air, and assure you that we have had nothing to do with the Denis Law business being dragged out,' he told me. 'Yes, we would like to sign him, but we have no intention of doing anything shady.'

I was pleased that the chairman of Juventus had taken such trouble to let us know how matters stood from his side, and returned to England feeling that, in the end, I would succeed in my quest. Two weeks later Torino had apparently reached the same conclusion, for Gigi Peronace called me—and this time, I wasn't being asked to trek across Europe. Instead, Gigi would come to see me. 'I've got full authority to negotiate the deal,' he assured me. And so Denis Law signed for Manchester United. The price: £115,000.

As I have already mentioned, at one stage in his subsequent career at Old Trafford Denis decided he should have a better contract. I received the request in the form of a letter. Actually, it read more like a demand, for there was a clear inference that if Denis didn't get what he was seeking, he was ready to leave United.

I had to ask myself: 'Does he mean it, or is he bluffing?' And I decided that in any event, there could be only one answer. I told my board: 'I don't believe we should give way . . . if Denis Law isn't satisfied with his terms, then we should put him on the transfer list.'

I sent for Denis and told him that in view of his letter, he was up for sale—and discovered that indeed I had called his bluff, for Denis himself ended the stalemate by phoning me and saying that he had simply been trying to do the best he could for himself. For which I didn't blame him.

My reply, though, was that we had done our best for him, and that if an apology were called for, it was not to me but to the public. Denis was big enough to admit that he had been in the wrong, and he stayed with United.

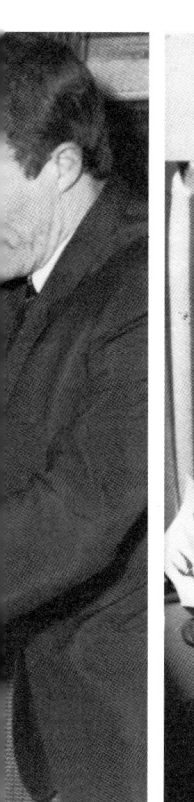

CTION—and re-
xation. Right, Denis
aw, in Scotland's col-
rs, faces up to Northern
eland's Terry Neill.
op left, Denis and for-
er Manchester City
am-mate Mike Sum-
erbee enjoy a laugh while
ocking down a pile of
nnies . . . and above,
avelling with Harry
regg and David Herd on
otball business for Man-
ester United.

95

ABOVE, the action at Old Trafford at the start of season 1967–68; and right, Matt Busby's message in the club's match programme on the eve of another European Cup campaign, which began with a tie against Hibernians, of Malta. The trail was to end at Wembley.

THE MAGNIFICENT OBSESSION

YUGOSLAVIA never became my favourite country, as far as football was concerned. For a start, it was on the way back from Belgrade that we became victims of the Munich disaster; for another thing, it was in Belgrade that we suffered a reverse which sickened us; and third, it was in Yugoslavia that I encountered my worst footballing experience. Let me hasten to add that I am not for one moment laying any blame at the door of the Yugoslavs, who always gave Manchester United a warm welcome.

Quite simply, your feelings about people and places tend to become coloured by your experiences with them, and—taking the third item first—I remember United playing Sarajevo in a European tie and fearing for the safety, if not the lives, of the match officials.

MATT BUSBY
TALKING

This season — as all our supporters are well aware — we are again competing in the European Cup and our initial opponents will be Hibernians, the Champions of Malta where, I am happy to say we have many friends and fans.

Indeed, the George Cross Island sports a Manchester United Supporters Club whose members will be eagerly looking forward to our visit on the 27th September when we play the second leg of the tie at the Gzira Stadium.

The first leg will be here at home a week earlier and we all hope you will, as always, give us the benefit of your support as we again attempt to bring the European Cup to England for the first time.

So far the honour has eluded us, although this winter, with your all-important vocal encouragement, we aim to go all out to claim soccer's richest prize to add to the League Championship we proudly won last season.

This evening, we have our first taste of international football in 1967–68 with the visit of a

The home supporters got carried away to the point almost of hysteria, and this seemed to have spread to some of the club officials by half-time. Not only did they blame the referee and his linesmen for having allowed a United goal to stand, but, as the teams and officials went in for the interval, they were after the men in black and . . . so I thought, for a few moments . . . after me.

Gesturing wildly and shouting vehemently, they were clearly in a mood to follow up with physical action, and the referee and his colleagues were horror-stricken. I wasn't feeling so brave myself, but I

THE EAGLES OF LISBON AND THEIR TROPHIES

ABOVE, the men of Benfica—the Eagles of Lisbon—who followed Real Madrid as kings of the European Cup, with two triumphs in the competition. Benfica won the trophy in seasons 1960–61 and 1961–62, and went to the final in 1963, narrowly missing out on a hat-trick. On the left, reminders of their double European Cup success.

THE SETTING FOR A DRAMATIC SEMI-FINAL

BELOW, the magnificent Bernabeu stadium, home of the great Real Madrid, who won the European Cup during five successive years (1956–1960). This stadium was the setting for a dramatic semi-final against Manchester United in 1968, as United beat Real to march on to Wembley and a confrontation with Benfica.

EXTRACTS from Matt Busby's columns in the United Review, as season 1967–68 progressed towards an unforgettable climax.

A GAMBLE THAT FAILED . . . BUT THERE WERE NO REAL EXCUSES

managed to put myself between the match officials and the ranting Yugoslavs, and finally the atmosphere cooled, although I could tell that our hosts were still simmering with indignation. Still, at least they had gone off the boil, and fortunately there were no second-half incidents to start another feud, although after the game the fans gave Manchester United a hot and hostile reception as we left the ground.

My second memory of Yugoslavia is of a European Cup semi-final United played against Partizan in 1966. And to this day I am convinced that we should have won the European Cup that year—which would have been 12 months before Glasgow Celtic became the first British club to achieve the distinction.

Really, there were no excuses, and we knew it, even though we took a calculated gamble by playing George Best—with a knee heavily bandaged—against Partizan in the first leg in Belgrade. The gamble failed, because by the end of the match we knew that George was booked for a cartilage operation (something we had suspected for a week or two previously) and we had conceded two goals without scoring, against a side which was inferior to Manchester United.

It was a game of two halves: in the first, Partizan seemed mesmerised merely by our reputation, and they played as if they expected to be hammered out of sight. Yet United simply didn't click, and it was no

score at the interval. In the second half, it was as if someone had convinced Partizan they were playing mere mortals, after all—and they came out to score twice, while we still couldn't find the net.

Among my memories of that match is an occasion when George Best did the three-card trick and teed up a chance for Denis Law—and Denis, standing almost under the bar, managed to head the ball over.

When I saw one of football's most lethal marksmen fluff a chance like that, my heart sank and I sensed it was going to be one of those days. Even though we tried to tell ourselves we would murder Partizan in the return at Old Trafford, we were all sick at heart because we knew we had passed up a glorious opportunity of nailing them on their own pitch. And when they came to Old Trafford, they took their courage in both hands and scraped through on aggregate. So they went to the final against Real Madrid—and, as we had foreseen, Partizan lost.

To make matters worse, United lost an F.A. Cup semi-final all in the same week, as Everton scored the only goal of the game at Burnden Park. Little wonder that the following Monday as I drove to Old Trafford, I was feeling bitterly disillusioned about the cruel blows of Soccer fate, and even Paddy Crerand's brave words after we had gone out of the European Cup seemed empty.

Paddy had tried to console me with: 'Don't worry,

EUROPEAN CHAMPIONS CUP COMPETITION

NINEPENCE **27**

APRIL 24 1968
KICK-OFF 7-45 P.M.
OLD TRAFFORD
MANCHESTER

SEMI FINAL

UNITED REVIEW

THE OFFICIAL PROGRAMME OF MANCHESTER UNITED FOOTBALL CLUB

MANCHESTER UNITED V **REAL MADRID**

Of all our opponents in Europe, Real Madrid probably stand alone for their sportsmanship on the field and their lavish hospitality before and after our various meetings.

They are, without doubt, the best-known club in Europe and they have a record unequalled in the premier tournament, the European Cup, for since its inception **they have never failed to qualify.**

It goes without saying too that Real have never failed to entertain; that they have received wonderful service from world-class stars such as Gento, Di Stefano, Puskas, Santamaria and many more and that they have always appeared able to produce the new faces at just the right time in every season.

Today, the Di Stefano-Puskas era is over and a "new" Real Madrid will be seen in action here at Old Trafford tonight, a side still steeped in the rich tradition that has been developed by Europe's greatest club.

We are extremely proud to be their hosts this evening and I know you will do your best to make them feel welcome – an experience that has always been ours whenever we have been in the magnificent Estadio Santiago Bernabeu ground or, indeed, in Madrid itself.

We are all fully aware of the greatness of which Real have proved themselves capable in the past and this evening I am certain we can look forward to a highly rewarding match in keeping with past meetings between the clubs and performances in keeping with all that is best in Europe's major club tournament.

A NOTABLE night for Manchester United (above, left), mirrored by the front cover of their match programme for the semi-final of the European Cup against Real Madrid at Old Trafford. Above, what Matt Busby had to say in his programme notes that night . . . and below, his promise that United will make a fight of it in the return game.

Our two most recent results – against Real Madrid in the European Cup and at West Bromwich in the League on Monday – mirror the ups and downs of football fortune as this season draws to a close.

What they mean, of course, is a wonderfully exciting finish to this campaign both at home and abroad; a wind-up that should provide all our supporters with an entertaining and exhilarating last three matches.

We will go to Spain for our second leg meeting with Real with a one-goal advantage. This barely reflected our superiority territorially over our semi-final opponents in the first match, but we got few of the right sort of breaks in front of goal.

I feel most of those who saw the game will agree with that point of view and, understandably, our boys will do everything in their power to add to our lead or defend it resolutely in our second meeting with Real in a bid to become the first English team to figure in a European Cup Final.

The result at West Brom was naturally

boss . . . we'll win it for you next year.' This year? Next year? Some time? Never . . . That was my mood as I drove towards Old Trafford. Then I saw a crocodile of children from a local school for the blind being led across the road and, as I pulled up to let them pass, I found my mood changing.

There was I, down in the mouth about some adverse results in the game of football, and there were those kids, unable to see and facing a lifetime like that . . . As I sat and watched them, my despair lifted and I told myself: 'Get your priorities right, Matt. At least you can do something about the European Cup!'

Frankly, ever since my wife, Jean, had told me in the Munich hospital that she felt sure the lads who had died would have wanted me to carry on, I had become increasingly obsessed about United winning the European Cup. It was almost as if this glittering trophy were the Holy Grail.

Well, in 1967 Glasgow Celtic beat us to the punch,

REAL BAR THE WAY—BUT I REMAIN CONVINCED WE CAN GO ON . . . TO BEAT BENFICA

SPORT LISBOA E BENFICA

LISBOA-PORTUGAL

but one year later the magnificent obsession became translated into achievement, as Manchester United overcame both Real Madrid and Benfica, who had both been giants of the competition, to accomplish the ultimate triumph.

In the first round, United had relatively little to beat, for the opposition came from Malta. In the second round, we tried conclusions with Sarajevo—a place really at the back of beyond, surrounded by mountains and, at that time, not on the list for scheduled flights. So, for the first time since Munich, United chartered an aircraft. We hired a BAC 111 for the round trip of something like 3,000 miles—and, as I have recalled, at half-time in the away leg there was that frightening experience concerning the match officials.

The next round took United into Poland, to play Gornik, and after we had taken a 2–0 lead at Old Trafford, we faced a return game in Arctic conditions. The pitch was covered with snow and ice, and flakes of snow were falling as the game got under way. Frankly, I felt so strongly that it could become a game of chance that I went to see the referee and express my views.

However, for some reason which was never made apparent, the referee appeared to be invisible—certainly I couldn't track him down until the game was almost due to start. So I shrugged my shoulders and hoped for the best. Twenty minutes from time, Lubanski scored for Gornik, and it needed a disciplined display by United to hang on to that by-now slender 2–1 overall lead. We did it, though, and we were through to the semi-finals, after having played on a sand-and-lime pitch in sunny Malta, survived the wrath of fans and home officials in Sarajevo, and come through on an ice-pack of a pitch in Poland.

This afternoon sees the end of another Football League season here at Old Trafford – and what a momentous finale fate has provided in the annual battle for the First Division Championship!

We are assured of the tightest, most thrilling climax to a campaign for some years, involving ourselves and our old and respected rivals from Maine Road, who also complete their programme today.

City have certainly had a fine season. They have been in touch with the leaders for some time now and following their excellent win at Tottenham a week ago and our victory against Newcastle the two clubs had level points after 41 matches.

With goal average a possibly decisive factor, both teams will be anxiously awaiting news from St. James's Park and Old Trafford as indeed will supporters in the two centres and those of Leeds and Liverpool who have been directly concerned with the destination of the Championship.

So the last day of the season in the League will be a truly memorable one and no matter what the outcome I wish to take this opportunity of congratulating all our fans for their considerable support in our efforts to provide the best in terms of soccer entertainment.

The players, I can assure you, are deeply appreciative of the vocal encouragement you have given them, especially in a season when we have been plagued by injuries to key members of the side.

Our thanks to you all, and I know you will offer a sincere and warm welcome on this final day of the season to our visitors Sunderland, and to their many followers who have travelled here for this match.

I meant it when I told my players: 'I have a feeling that this will be our year . . .'

For the fourth time, Manchester United had reached the semi-finals of the European Cup and—not for the first time—Real Madrid barred the way. But my conviction that we could overcome the great Spanish team remained, and I also felt that if we did, we need not fear our opponents in the final—who, in my view, would turn out to be Benfica.

100

ABOVE, the magnificent display of trophies on show at the headquarters of Benfica, the Eagles of Lisbon, whom Manchester United were destined to meet in the 1968 final of the European Cup.

It was a season which ended in a double drama, for United were pipped at the post for a second successive League title—and by their great rivals, Manchester City. As Matt Busby said in his notes for the final League game (far left), fate had provided a momentous finale. In the event, United faltered against Sunderland, City won at Newcastle . . . and took the title by two points.

THE MAN WITH THE GOLDEN BOOT . . .

THE ace in Benfica's pack . . . Eusebio, the star who packed a lethal shot. Manchester United were to face him in the final of the European Cup in 1968—and only a brilliant save by 'keeper Alex Stepney denied Eusebio a goal.

Eusébio

TRIUMPHANT AT WEMBLEY IN 1968 . . . VIA MADRID

O N 20 April 1968, Manchester United played Sheffield United in a League match, and won 1–0. Denis Law was the marksman, but neither he nor anyone else was feeling sanguine about the victory. Denis had been plagued with knee trouble, United had played in fits and starts . . . and four days later we were due to meet Real Madrid in the first leg of the European Cup semi-final.

The team against Sheffield United had read: Stepney; Brennan, Dunne; Crerand, Sadler, Stiles; Best, Kidd, Charlton, Law, Aston. Bill Foulkes had been missing from the line-up, and there was speculation whether or not he would be back for the European tie, while for Denis that League game was the final test of fitness. Our hard-won victory against The Blades also produced one or two knocks for other players—notably Best and Charlton—and it seemed as if the team for the match against Real Madrid was in the melting pot.

Real no longer had Di Stefano or Puskas, and they were without Amancio (through suspension), while De Felipe had succeeded the great Santamaria at centre-half. But they still had Gento, and in Pirri and Zocco they had other world-class stars.

When the game began, Law, Charlton and Best were there, but Bill Foulkes wasn't in United's line-up. Real and United sparred warily in the early stages, but after 35 minutes 63,000 fans were on their feet as winger John Aston won the ball from Gonzales and crossed it for Best, standing 15 yards out, to hit it on the half-volley with his left foot. 'Keeper Betancort must have seen just a blur as the ball sped past him.

Betancort earned his wages, though, with a series of scintillating saves, especially when, in the last quarter of an hour, he foiled Aston of a goal, and so Real kept the score down to 1–0. It was a trifling lead to take to Madrid, but we could do no more..

United had two changes for the return: Denis Law, still feeling that injury, was a spectator, and Bill Foulkes was back to reinforce the defence, with David Sadler doubling as defender and, whenever possible, as an attacker.

CUPS AT LAST

ON THE ROAD TO GLORY

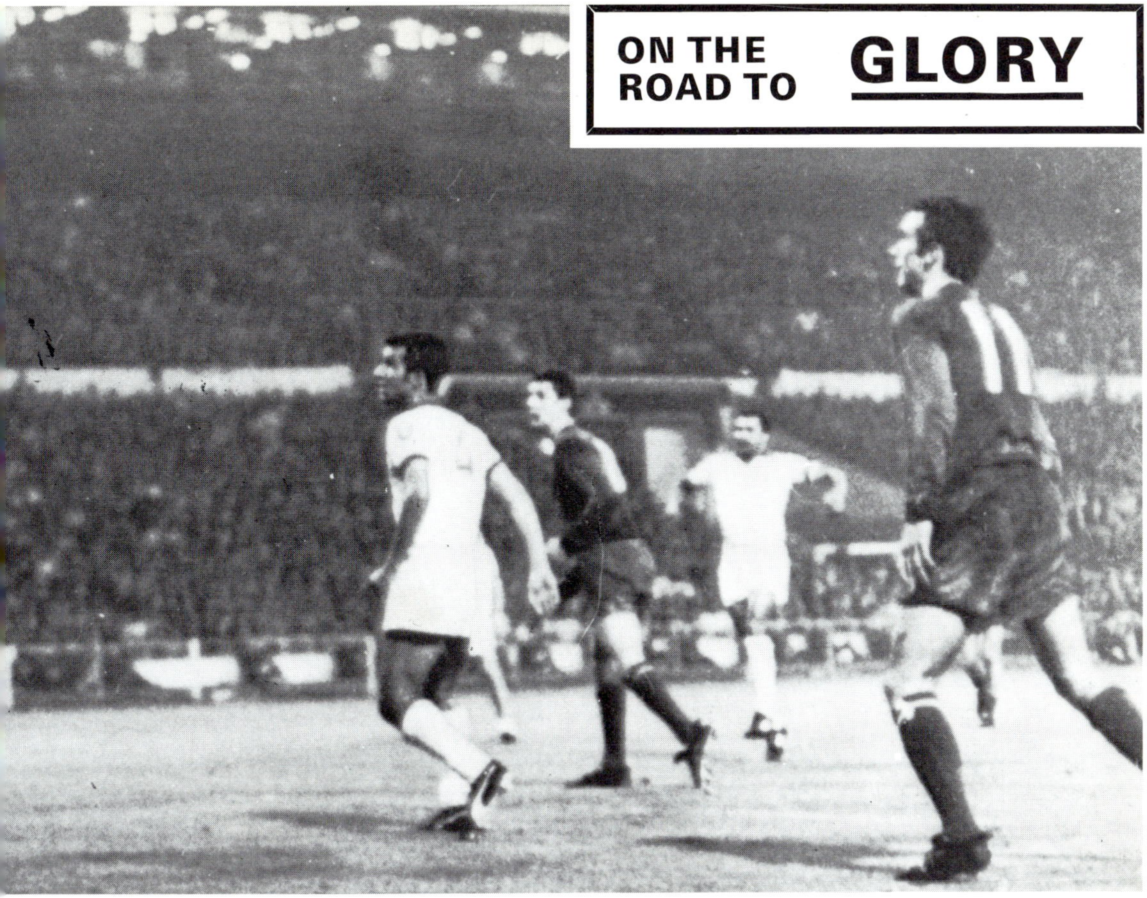

THE 1968 European Cup final, and Brian Kidd (in centre) scores 'United's third goal, with Benfica 'keeper Jose Hénriques leaping in vain as the ball scorches past him. Left, John Aston, the winger who played the game of his life for United on European Cup-final night at Wembley— holds the gleaming trophy aloft.

AT LAST, the European Cup has landed at Old Trafford, and everyone at United has a share in the glory, as the players, manager Matt Busby, directors and club officials take their places in front of the camera for an historic picture.

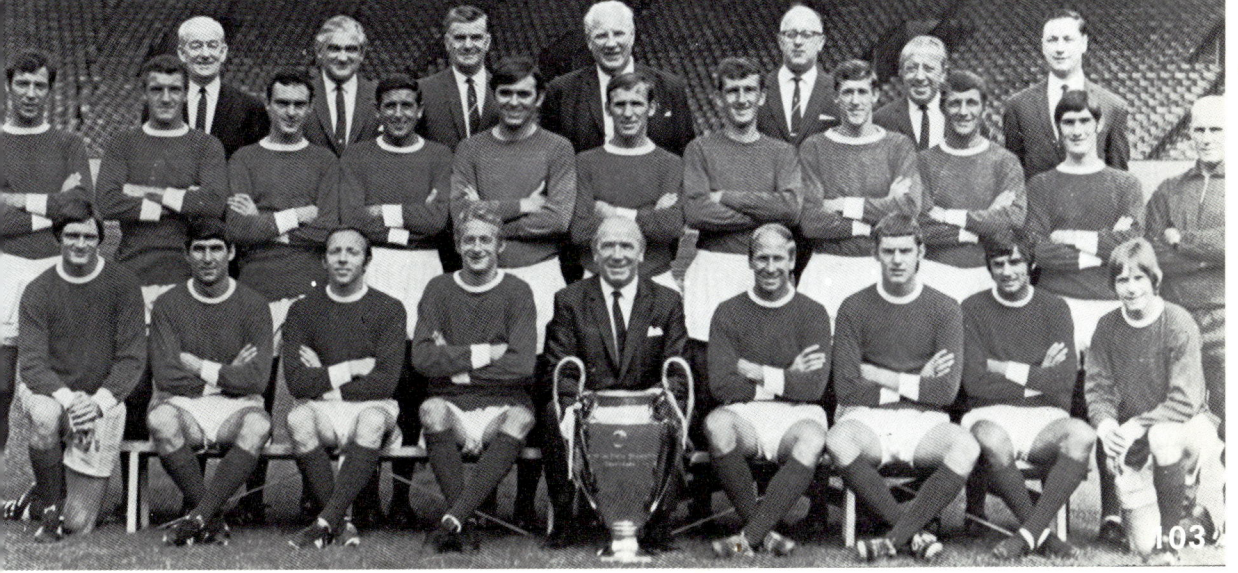

It was Real who attacked from the start, and 15 minutes before half-time they breached United's defence. They scored . . . then scored again . . . and struck a third goal, while—thanks to Zocco, who put through his own goal—United got their names on the scoresheet once.

At half-time, heads were down in the United dressing-room, and I wasn't feeling at my happiest. What was there to say? I pondered, then came up with the answer. I rammed it home at my lads: 'Look, we're losing, but it's still only 3–2 on aggregate. If we're going to go down, let's go down making a fight of it! We might as well lose 6–2 as 3–2.'

Outside, 120,000 fans were prepared to see Real continue the slaughter, but I had managed to pick my players up from the floor, and they went out determined to act on my words.

George Best set the team alight when he got the ball and wove a way through, then crossed for David Sadler to apply the finishing touch. That made it 3–3, and gave us a chance of a play-off in a neutral country . . . but the greatest drama was yet to come, for again Best made the running, again he got the ball into Real's goalmouth—and Bill Foulkes, the man whose job it was to prevent goals, was up in attack to side-foot the ball into the net.

That left Real with it all to do, and fewer than 15 minutes in which to do it. Those 120,000 spectators had gone deadly quiet, as Real tried to earn a play-off. But deep down, I sensed that, at last, we were not to be denied a place in the final. And we were not.

As the teams trooped off the pitch, I went to greet my players and I am not ashamed to say that tears of joy were coursing down my face. It was an emotional moment for all of us, especially for the lads who, like myself, had been chasing the elusive target of the European Cup since Munich. We still had one hurdle to surmount, but we knew it couldn't be any more formidable than Real Madrid. And the final against Benfica would be at Wembley.

I took the team down to Egham, for their stay at the pre-match headquarters, and we all tried to relax. Easier said than done, but the day of the game finally arrived. I won't say the side picked itself, because Denis Law must have been in, had he been fully fit; instead, he was in hospital as a result of that knee trouble. Up front for United was Brian Kidd. It was his 19th birthday . . .

There were 100,000 people at Wembley, the referee was an Italian, Concetto Lo Bello, and United

BILL FOULKES . . . marksman whose goal against Real Madrid put United into the European Cup final.

were set to take on the Eagles of Lisbon, Eusebio and all. The first half was something of a let-down, apart from a heart-stopping moment when Eusebio let fly and his shot rattled the bar. A lucky escape for United.

At half-time it was still 0–0, but eight minutes after the restart it was 1–0 for United with Bobby Charlton—not noted for heading the ball—nodding it home. Victory was within our grasp, but I could see the tension taking its toll as the minutes ticked away, and it didn't surprise me when Benfica equalised, for

European Cup Winners 1968

European Cup Semi-Finalists
1957 1958 1966

First Division League Champions
1908 1911 1952 1956 1957 1965 1967
Runners-up
1947 1948 1949 1951 1959 1964 1968

Second Division League Champions
1936. Runners-up 1897 1906 1925 1938

F.A. Cup Winners 1909 1948 1963
Finalists 1957 1958

F.A. Charity Shield Winners
1908 1911 1953 1957 1958
Joint Winners   Finalists
1965 1967   1949 1963

F.A. Youth Cup Winners
1953 1954 1955 1956 1957 1964

Inter Cities Fairs Cup Semi-Finalists 1965

World Club Championship Finalists 1968

MATT BUSBY with the trophy; and left, Bobby Charlton, who stole quietly away to bed after United's Wembley triumph.

they had been pushing forward and threatening to score.

Shortly after Graca's goal, Eusebio broke through, and everything pointed to him scoring. I was so certain it was going to be a goal that I was saying to myself, 'Oh, no ... Not again.' I could see the European Cup being snatched from us as Eusebio escaped from Nobby Stiles for virtually the only time in the game. I knew Eusebio's finishing power, and when he broke clear, with only Alex Stepney to beat, I simply couldn't see the Benfica man missing.

The ball left Eusebio's foot like a bullet from a high-velocity rifle, and it sped towards the target with deadly accuracy. United's 'keeper was moving, too, as he dived desperately to get to the ball, but even as I anticipated it speeding past him, somehow he had clawed it to safety, and United had staged their great escape.

Just before the whistle signalled the end of 90 minutes, I was feeling that Manchester United were still not out of the wood, since it appeared to me that in the final period we had been losing our way, giving the Benfica players room and allowing them to win the ball. So during the brief respite I urged my men: 'Just don't give the ball away!' My experience of Wembley had taught me that this is a failing which can be fatal. My parting shot was: 'When you make a pass, make sure it reaches your team-mate.'

United's players heeded my words—and they did more. They raised their game again, and George Best was the man who turned it on and did the damage, as he took the ball up to the 'keeper, Henriques, drew him out, then rounded him and slipped the ball over the line to make it 2–1.

Brian Kidd celebrated his birthday by making it 3–1, then made a goal for Bobby Charlton, and then I knew that nothing was going to stop Manchester United winning the European Cup. As I realised this, the thought flashed through my mind: 'This is what we set out to do . . . this is what it was all about.' There were still five minutes to go, but I was certain nothing

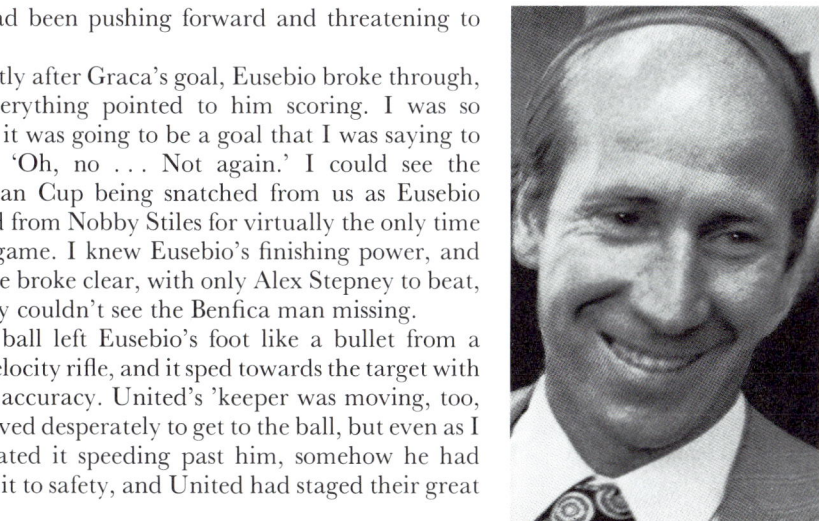

would go wrong, and it didn't.

Tears rolled down my cheeks as I embraced players, and there was a lump in my throat as I put my arms around Bobby Charlton, one of the Munich survivors. It had been a 10-year trek from that snowswept airstrip to Wembley, but we had made it all the way and, ultimately, overcome heartbreaks and setbacks to score a decisive triumph.

In a way, I felt drained; yet I knew that sleep would elude me that night, because there was so much to think about. There was a reception for both teams at Wembley, and Benfica were sportingly ungrudging in their attitude towards our success. It was a night to be savoured, a night to go out on the town, and when I did retire the dawn was not far distant. And for one man, the occasion had proved too much . . . for Bobby Charlton, who had written his name into the books as a truly great player, left Wembley stadium not to carry on celebrating, but to return to the team's hotel and steal quietly away to bed.

ONCE I saw George Best raise the roof with his trickery during a five-a-side game. On other occasions he certainly raised my blood pressure and, now and then, I think we both had sleepless nights. Yet I was lucky, because George's escapades during his days with Manchester United began after I had had the greatest seasons of his career from him and while I was coming towards the close of my own spell as manager.

The five-a-side game sticks in my mind. George simply toe-ended the ball against his opponent's shin, then hit the rebound cleanly and clinically past the goalkeeper. It was a deliberate piece of artistry few could have matched.

George was a manager's dream and nightmare all rolled into one. He turned out to be a wayward genius, and I am not going to attempt to catalogue the incidents which made headline news before he shook the dust of Old Trafford from his feet. It's common knowledge that he missed trains and training, that his off-the-field adventures created problems as well.

My thoughts go back to his earliest days, when George burst upon the Soccer scene like a new comet in the sky. It was obvious that here was a talent which would take football by storm. I recall him playing against Burnley at Old Trafford, against Southampton at The Dell and—best of all—against Chelsea at Stamford Bridge.

Ken Shellito was Chelsea's right-back, George Best was United's outside-left . . . and Best mesmerised the Chelsea man. It must have been soul-destroying for Shellito as this kid produced every Soccer trick in the book, and many tricks that had never been in it. the place erupted, and George's name was on everyone's lips as the game came to a close.

I remember his name being on another man's lips during a tour of the Far East. We played a New Zealand Select at Christchurch, and there were around 20,000 people watching. I think the final score was 5–0 or 6–0 for United, with George hitting a hat-trick, and immediately behind me one of the New Zealand selectors sat . . . with his head in his hands for most of the match.

He raised the roof with his Soccer trickery . . . other times he raised blood pressure

GEORGE BEST was once a shy, retiring young Irish boy who spent most of his evenings listening to records in his digs after training in the day with Manchester United. Now he has become the darling of the gossip columnists.

MILLIONS of words have been written about George Best, the unknown from Belfast who became a Soccer superstar. And these words (above and below) were penned in a souvenir programme when Manchester United toured Australia in 1967. Matt Busby recalls the days of Best at Old Trafford . . . 'he became very difficult to handle . . . but I cannot forget that he gave us six years before things turned really sour.'

Matt Busby quickly realised that there was little he could teach the young Irish boy and encouraged him to play it by ear once he got on to the field. It was not long before Best was becoming the terror of opposing full-backs and he was awarded his first full international cap for Northern Ireland when still only 18. And even now he is only 21 . . .

GEORGE BEST

He gave us six years before things went sour

I kept hearing him say: 'Oh, no . . . he's got it again . . .' Meaning George and the ball.

There was the European tie in Portugal against Benfica when United, going out with a slender lead, produced a magnificent display to score five goals. We had all gone out there knowing we would have our hands full with Eusebio and company, but during the first half Best did everything. I think he scored two or three of our goals—certainly he turned on his own distinctive brand of Soccer magic in what, for me, was probably the finest display I have ever seen from him.

In one move he collected the ball, pulled it back, dummied and then scored . . . and for Benfica, it got progressively worse. That was the night he got the name 'El Beatle'.

Best the problem boy? Yes, he became very difficult to handle. But I cannot forget that he gave us six years before things turned really sour.

LEFT, a boyish-looking George Best—and alongside, the figure who became familiar in the red jersey of Manchester United. Below, the European Cup is on its way to Old Trafford, and 'keeper Hénriques dives too late to prevent United's second goal. The scorer: George Best.

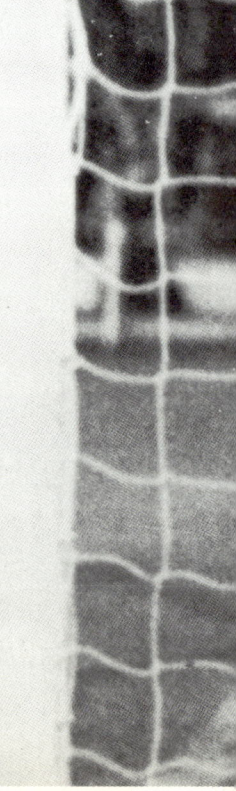

THE MAN THEY CAME TO KNOW AS 'EL BEATLE'

Girls in Lisbon screamed "El Beatle" every time he got the ball when he inspired Manchester United to thrash Benfica by 5-1 in a European Champions' Cup match. After the game a man came at him with a knife—to hack off a lock of hair as a souvenir.

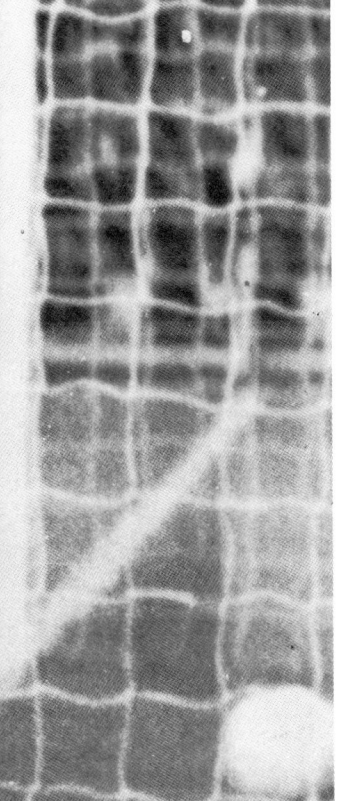

AN auspicious moment in George Best's career, as he wins the coveted European Footballer of the Year award, with Bobby Charlton, Matt Busby and Denis Law gracing the occasion.

TEARS WOULD RUN DOWN HIS FACE, AS HE MADE WHAT WAS MEANT TO BE A LASTING PROMISE

I used to call him into my office and play hell with him about some of the misdemeanours he had perpetrated. Often he reassured me, 'It won't happen again', and occasionally tears ran down his face as he made what, at the time, was meant to be a lasting promise.

For a couple of months, maybe, he would be a reformed character, good as gold and shunning the bright lights and any hint of wrong company. More than once, I warned him that he was heading for self-destruction.

Little-boy lost? That was how he seemed to me sometimes, for when he was behaving himself he was such a likeable lad, so quietly spoken that it seemed butter wouldn't melt in his mouth. He was indeed a jumble of contradictions.

Once we went together to a school where the kids besieged him with requests for autographs and pleas to be photographed standing next to him. He obliged to the point where, patient as I consider myself to be, I protested: 'That's enough . . . it's going on too long.' Yes, George had so many good qualities.

What really went wrong? I don't believe even George knows, and the only theory I can put forward is that possibly fame came too swiftly for him to handle. I used to worry about him and, now and again, lose sleep over him. I also told myself: 'You can try to help, you can try to guide him and have other

> Already he has won recognition as one of the most brilliant young players in the world.
> "It's hard to believe that one boy can be blessed with so much talent, and that fate will not take some sort of quick revenge on him," wrote Danny Blanchflower recently in the Sunday Express.

people watching over him . . . but you can't live with the lad 24 hours a day.'

Whenever I challenged him about one of his escapades, I was offered that 'it won't happen again'. And he meant it. I used to say to him: 'For goodness' sake, why don't you settle down and get married to a nice girl, instead of fooling around?'

When United returned from a trip to Scandinavia, there were headlines about a girl he had met and, apparently, was going to marry. I hadn't been on that trip and I hauled him up to the office to ask him what he thought he was playing at.

His answer: 'You're always on at me about getting married . . . now that's what I'm going to do.'

I countered by saying that I didn't expect him to wed a lass he'd known for only a couple of weeks.

That romance fizzled out before long.

I never really knew what was going on in George's head and, I suspect, he wasn't very sure himself at times. I believe that he had a handful of close friends who were good for him and did their best for him, but I'm certain there were many hangers-on who, in the end, helped to destroy his career in top-class football here.

GOALMOUTH action—and George Best almost gets his name on the scoresheet in a game against Liverpool.

> Best's superb control, balance and fine acceleration are added to the courage both to beat bigger men and challenge them in circumstances where he might get hurt. The way he taunts a rival defender is both calculated and precocious.

MORE of the quotes about Best, when he made such an impact on Manchester United's tour of Australia in 1967. By then, he had become a household name around the world.

> The sight of Best's frail looking figure conjuring the ball away from a rival defender with magic dexterity is enough to send any soccer fan away from the ground bubbling with excitement.
> He is the star of Northern

> Ireland's national team and not even the brilliance of Denis Law or the genius of Bobby Charlton can push the young Irishman into the background when Manchester United are playing

One thing that saddened me was that George's antics were not affecting only the image of a Soccer superstar, a footballer who, in my view, was unique. They were not good for the image of Manchester United either.

Inevitably, there came the parting of the ways between George and Manchester United. That was a sad day for me, too, because I couldn't help remembering the lad who had arrived at Old Trafford even as I shook my head about the scrapes he had got into at the club and outside it.

Eventually, George did get married, and I read about his romance. I even met George and his wife, Angie, after he had returned from playing in America—and I must say that he struck me then as being very conscious of all the problems he had caused me during his time at United. In fact, I felt that he felt he had done some stupid and unnecessary things . . . but I still couldn't fathom what made him tick.

I have to say, also, that of all the truly great players who passed through my hands as a manager, George

Best was the one who gave me the most enjoyment— as a footballer. There was a charisma about him that made him something special and made me, as a follower of football, never mind as a manager, tingle with a feeling of expectation whenever he got the ball.

I am not belittling the qualities of any other player when I say that George had something which put him in a class apart.

I do know that he has earned a great deal of money through the years, and I sincerely hope that he has looked after a goodly part of it. I shall always believe that George Best should have become the first footballer to make a million pounds, for the opportunities were there for him, on and off the field.

If he did, good luck to him : and if he didn't . . . ah, well. And there I go, shaking my head again.

111

UNITED aces in international action (right): Jackie Blanchflower and Harry Gregg (Northern Ireland) and Tommy Taylor (England). Below right: Alex Stepney, Matt Busby's choice as last line of defence.

ON the left, Johnny Carey . . . inspiring skipper and player supreme; on the right, Charlie Mitten . . . pin-point crosser of a ball and scorer of 'cheeky' goals.

UNITED ALL-STARS

TWO DOZEN ACES AND MORE . . . BUT IN THE END, THIS WAS MY LINE-UP:

STEPNEY

CAREY   BYRNE
CHILTON EDWARDS

CRERAND   BEST
CHARLTON

LAW   TAYLOR   MITTEN

Substitute:
VIOLLET

PROBLEMS, PROBLEMS— STARTING WITH A CHOICE BETWEEN STEPNEY AND GREGG

EVEN for Matt Busby, the task of picking an all-star Manchester United team presented problems, because inside 10 minutes I had assembled a list of more than two dozen contenders for places!

Scan through these names, and you will realise the difficulties I faced . . . Alex Stepney, Harry Gregg, Ray Wood, Jack Crompton, Johnny Carey, Bill Foulkes, Roger Byrne, Tony Dunne, Johnny Aston, Allenby Chilton, Mark Jones, Jackie Blanchflower, Duncan Edwards, Nobby Stiles, Henry Cockburn, Paddy Crerand, Eddie Colman, George Best, Johnny Berry, Jimmy Delaney, Bobby Charlton, Liam Whelan, Johnny Morris, Tommy Taylor, David Herd, Denis Law, Dennis Viollet, Stan Pearson, Jack Rowley, Charlie Mitten.

Take only the task of naming the goalkeeper. From four candidates, I whittled down the list to two. My short list? Alex Stepney and Harry Gregg, both of whom gave United tremendous service over a decade or more.

Finally, I pencilled in the name Stepney. Not merely because he made a brilliant save which contributed materially to United winning the 1968 European Cup final, but because, overall, I felt he was the type of 'keeper I could play in any and every match, irrespective of the occasion.

Consistency was Stepney's middle name. You knew exactly how he would do his job, and you could leave him to it. Very rarely did he make a mistake which led to a 'soft' goal, and he inspired confidence in the players in front of him.

Frankly, I had a hard time making my final choice, and Harry Gregg so nearly commanded a place. But I kept coming back to Alex Stepney, and so he goes in.

It was somewhat easier when I thought about right-back, for the original choice was between Johnny Carey and Bill Foulkes, so that narrowed the

ROGER BYRNE at the height of his career with United and England. Below: Tony Dunne and Bill Foulkes.

FAR right, Allenby Chilton, the centre-half who nursed the Busby babes along. Top right: Duncan Edwards, a giant in stature and as a footballer. Right: Jackie Blanchflower, who—like Dunne and Foulkes—staked a strong claim for inclusion in Matt Busby's all-star side.

FOUR CONTENDERS FOR THE No. 5 SHIRT: AND IT GOES TO CHILTON

field. Bill was a decisive player, and he didn't flinch from a tackle; but I feel that anyone who saw Carey at his peak would concede that in naming him, no explanation really was required.

However, I shall give one, and start by saying, quite simply, that Johnny Carey was one of the all-time greats among *all* the footballers I have seen. He never got ruffled, he was constructive, he read the game so well, he was a great influence as skipper, and he spoon-fed people who played in front of him because he was so creative. I have never seen a better right-back, and that just about says it all.

Left-back? It had to be between Roger Byrne, Tony Dunne and Johnny Aston—each man a great full-back, as well as a great professional. Indeed, if you had a Tony Dunne or a Johnny Aston as your first choice, you could consider yourself fortunate. Yet Roger Byrne had to get my vote. His speed was deceptive—he could recover instantly, although he was seldom beaten, and as a captain he played another part in the overall scheme of things. In short, he was another Carey. Enough said . . .

Had Eddie Colman lived longer, I might have ended up naming him for the right-half position, because little 'Snakehips' showed all the promise of eventual greatness. Tragically, Munich cut short Eddie's life. So I turned to the one other name which dominated my thoughts . . . Paddy Crerand.

People used to say that Paddy was slow and could be caught out. Maybe . . . but not often. When he played, so did United, and while one man doesn't make a team, I always felt that the Charltons, the Laws—yes, even the Bests—relied upon Paddy a great deal for their service. So in goes Crerand.

Bill Foulkes came into consideration again when I thought about the centre-half position. So did Mark Jones and Jackie Blanchflower. Foulkes and Jones were each resolute defenders; Blanchflower was more creative.

Well, three into one won't go—and I had four contenders for the No. 5 shirt. The fourth man got my

vote . . . Allenby Chilton, whose switch from wing-half to central defender saw him really hit the top. Nothing seemed to beat him in the air, and the longer he played, the better he seemed to get.

Chilton was truly a stalwart, and I don't mind confessing that when I realised he was coming towards the close of his career, I worried a bit about his successor. Even while he was still playing, and I was bringing in youngsters around him, he nursed them along, and I knew I could rely on him to make it easier for them while still coping with his own job.

Left-half? I've mentioned Nobby Stiles and Henry Cockburn, both great players in a club side because they worked so hard for the team and their enthusiasm rubbed off on to other people. They were on the small side, but their positional play was so good they never failed—and they both wanted to win.

Yet one player showed that, even as a teenager, he was a giant both in stature and ability . . . Duncan Edwards. You could have picked him for any position with absolute confidence and, indeed, when United were finding it hard at times to score goals, I used to push 'Big Dunc' forward and he would oblige.

He was like a tank as he bored his way through the middle, seemingly brushing aside the waves of

NO argument about one position in Matt Busby's all-star Manchester United side . . . a place just had to be found for George Best (left).

RIGHT, Paddy Crerand, the midfield man about whom it was said: 'When he's on song, so are Manchester United.' A verdict with which Matt Busby agrees.

AT his best in a deep-lying position, roaming around and linking up with people. And he could fire the ball like a bullet. That, of course, was Bobby Charlton.

BEST, BERRY AND DELANEY . . . BUT WHAT ABOUT MITTEN?

opposition, and he would finish off an attack with a powerful shot which often homed straight to the target. I don't believe anyone would argue with my choice of Duncan Edwards for the No. 6 jersey.

So I've named six players, and now it's a case of finding five more from a list of at least twice as many. I considered Johnny Berry for outside-right, and I considered Jimmy Delaney for the same position, with George Best on the left wing. So where did that leave Charlie Mitten?

I considered David Herd, Tommy Taylor, Bobby Charlton, Denis Law, Dennis Viollet, Stan Pearson, Johnny Morris, Liam Whelan, Jack Rowley . . . all these for the three remaining positions. Then I started all over again.

Best just had to have a place, and I gave him the No. 7 shirt. Here was a player who was more naturally gifted than any other footballer I've seen. He didn't even have to work at it, as so many footballers who have achieved success have had to do. Natural skill? He could dribble, pass, shoot, head the ball—and win it in a tackle. Like Carey, Byrne, Edwards, he was a 'must' for my team.

And the rest of my forward line finished up reading Charlton, Taylor, Law, Mitten—with apologies to the men I had omitted.

Charlton could play a variety of roles, but he was at his best in a deep-lying position, roaming around and linking up with people. His strength in shooting became famous, because he could hit the ball like a bullet. If Bobby had one flaw, it was in his heading, as he would be the first to admit—yet, as if to refute even this apparent slight weakness, he headed a goal in the European Cup final against Benfica.

At centre-forward I had to choose finally between Jack Rowley and Tommy Taylor. 'The Gunner' *was*

RIGHT, Jimmy Delaney, who turned out to be a bargain signing by Manchester United. And far right, Johnny Berry, who so often used to put it across United before he was signed from Birmingham.

LAW: HIS FRAME WAS SLIGHT, HIS SKILL AND COURAGE WERE BOUNDLESS

UNLUCKY not to a claim a place in the all-star side, but demanding inclusion as substitute . . . that's Dennis Viollet. He fills the bill as a man who could scheme in midfield and, when it mattered, as a striker who could rifle a goal.

a great centre-forward, and he might have packed a more lethal shot in his left foot than Taylor; but I don't feel that he was as commanding in the air.

Tommy seemed to climb, then hover in space. No wonder he won the ball almost every time. More than that, he was brilliant at nodding it precisely to a team-mate, whether it was sideways, forwards or even backwards. And he held the forward line together superbly.

When he nodded the ball, it went where he wanted it to go. He could shoot, as well. Yet he was unselfish— if someone else was in a better position, Tommy would supply him with the ammunition. In addition, he was the ideal man for a team-mate to ping the ball at . . . and inside the box he was devastating.

Inside-left inevitably brought up three names when it came to the short list for selection: Law, Viollet and Pearson. I found it difficult to pick one name and still not include the other two in my attack. Reluctantly, and somewhat sadly, I discarded the names of Viollet and Pearson . . . and that left Law.

Like Taylor, he was unselfish in setting up goals for team-mates; yet he had that killer instinct himself, and inside the six-yard box he was electric. He could score goals from impossible situations. He was brave to the point that he went in where, as they say, angels feared to tread, and he took so many knocks that at times I have seen his legs black and blue with bruises.

What made Denis all the more remarkable was that, really, there was nothing of him. His frame was slight, but his courage and ability were boundless. I often think of those photographs of him as a kid—yes, spectacles and all. A more unlikely-looking candidate for Soccer stardom you never saw.

And so to the last man in the line. 'Cheeky' Charlie

Mitten. We had to agree to differ when he went to Bogota, but that didn't mean I thought less of him as a player, and while he worked on the left side of the park, he careered in and out and often caused chaos among opposing defenders.

Crossing the ball, he made it look like a precision job as he invariably found his man; and when he cut inside and let fly with his left foot from 20 yards, his

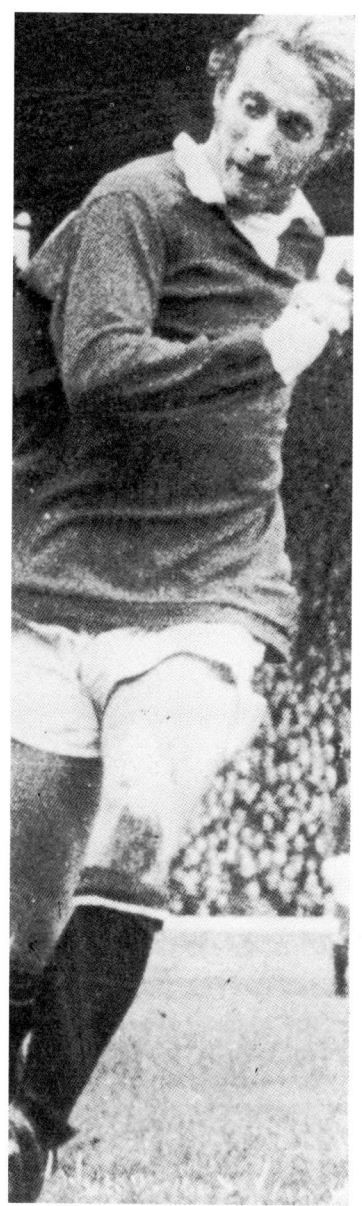

DENIS LAW . . . a player with the killer instinct. He could score from impossible situations—and above, he's showing that famed aerial power as he heads a great goal against Newcastle United at Old Trafford.

tell the 'keeper, each time he was taking the spot-kick: 'I'm going to put it there.' And he did just that, picking his spot each time and giving the 'keeper—despite that advance warning—not the ghost of a chance.

Finally, I decided I would have to name a substitute, and these names came to mind: Gregg, Foulkes, Dunne, Delaney, Berry, Pearson, Viollet, Colman, Cockburn, Stiles, Morris, Whelan.

It isn't usual to name a goalkeeper, so that cut the list by one; and at last I decided it must be a man who could operate in a dual role—scheming in midfield and, if need be, rifling a goal when it mattered. So it became a choice between Berry, Pearson and Viollet, and in the end, Dennis was my man.

Now I had my all-star Manchester United side: Stepney; Carey, Byrne; Crerand, Chilton, Edwards; Best, Charlton, Taylor, Law, Mitten. Substitute: Viollet. And I must admit that's a team I would love to have led out in an F.A. Cup final at Wembley . . .

aim was deadly. He was no ball-juggler, yet he earned his nickname of 'Cheeky Charlie' because of his immense confidence in himself. When you looked for a left-winger, he had all the qualities you sought.

My enduring memory of Charlie is of a hat-trick he scored from the penalty spot in a game at Old Trafford. He could hit the ball so cleanly, and he knew this . . . which was why he had the effrontery to

122

FROM the top (left): Ray Wilkins, Gordon McQueen, Lou Macari and Joe Jordan ... signings who cost United a combined total of around £1,850,000. Left, Steve Coppell, another signing—but he was a much more modest investment, in terms of cash. All are internationals.

TWO home-produced players (above), Northern Ireland internationals Jimmy Nicholl and Sammy McIlroy, and here is another star who cost United nothing ... goalkeeper Gary Bailey. Top right, Welsh international Mickey Thomas, a £350,000 investment from Wrexham.

UNITED STARS OF TODAY

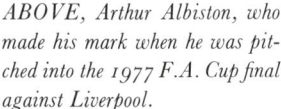

ABOVE, *Arthur Albiston, who made his mark when he was pitched into the 1977 F.A. Cup final against Liverpool.*

TWO Irish players who have given a good account of themselves ... Ashley Grimes (above) and Kevin Moran (right). On the left, Gordon McQueen in action.

UNITED skipper Martin Buchan, a Scotland international and a player who almost always produces an impeccable performance at the heart of the defence. Buchan seldom appears to be less than cool, calm and collected.

125

SOME YOU WIN . . .

LEFT, Brian Greenhoff is consoled by Tommy Cavanagh, after defeat in the 1976 F.A. Cup final against Southampton, while the disappointment shows in manager Tommy Docherty's face, too. Above, a different story after the 1977 Wembley victory over Liverpool, as The Doc. gives the thumbs-up and brothers Jimmy and Brian Greenhoff hold up the trophy. Right: Sammy McIlroy and Stuart Pearson give 'The Doc' a helping hand as United's players do a Wembley lap of honour.

AND SOME YOU LOSE

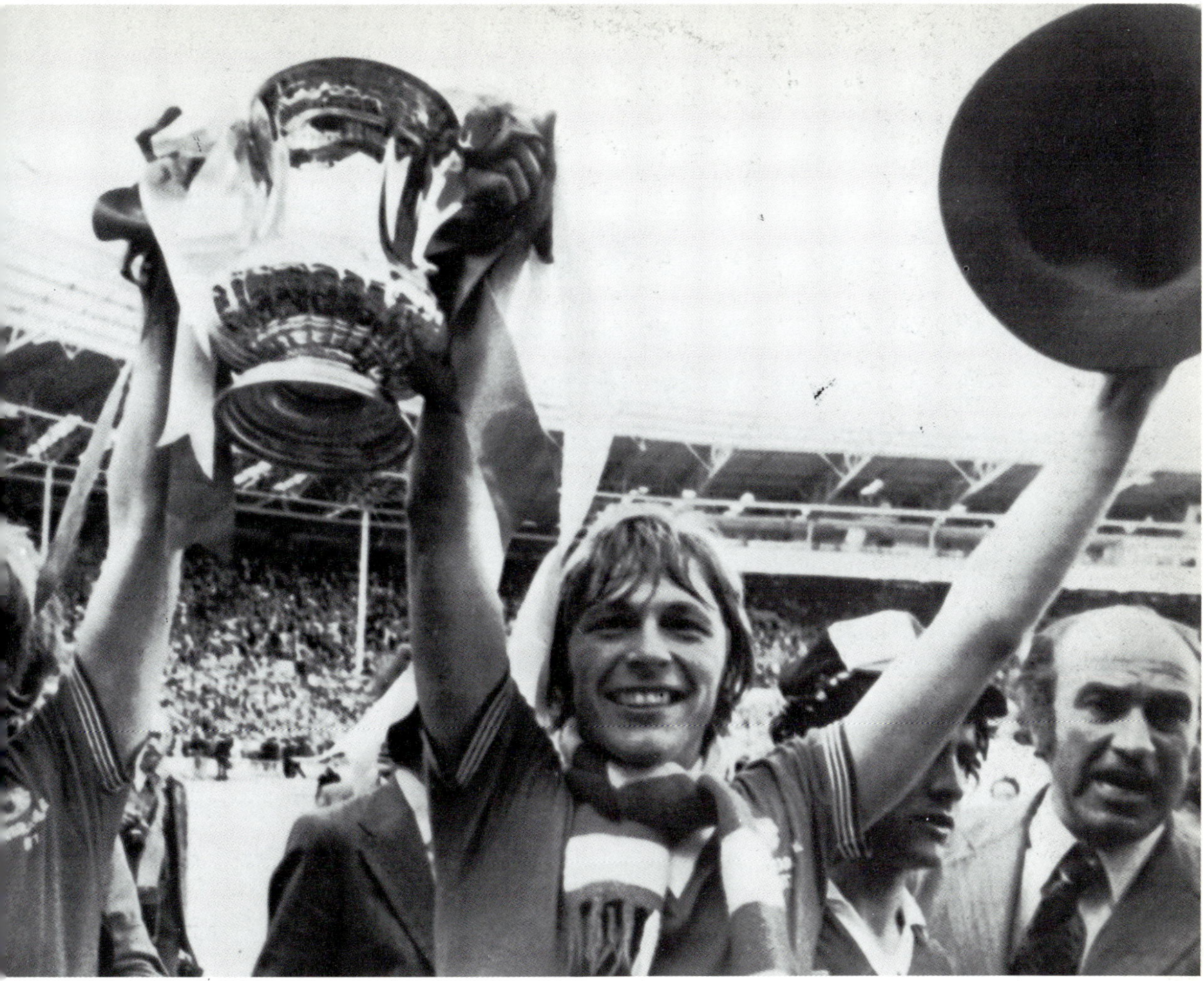

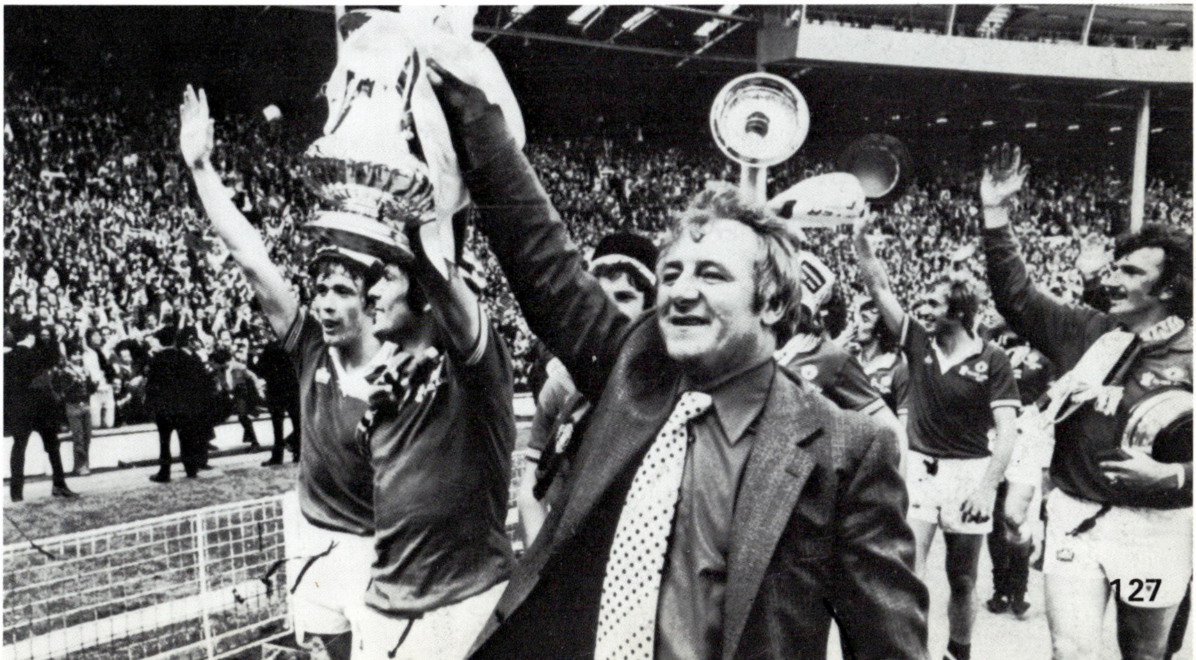

WINNING, SHARING . . . AND LOSING

ABOVE, United's 1977 F.A. Cup-final squad, complete with the trophy they won after beating Liverpool at Wembley. Right, a few months later and both clubs are back there, with Brian Greenhoff and Phil Thompson holding the Charity Shield, which Cup winners and League champions shared. Bottom right, a moment of triumph for United in the 1977 semi-final against Leeds at Hillsborough, as Jimmy Greenhoff (No. 8, and almost hidden on the far left) scores goal No. 1 for United in a crowded goalmouth.

BELOW, the 1976 F.A. Cup final between United and Southampton—and Sammy McIlroy (No. 8) comes so close to getting his name on the scoresheet for United. But his header hit the bar . . . and the Saints went on to win, 1—0, thanks to a goal by Bobby Stokes.

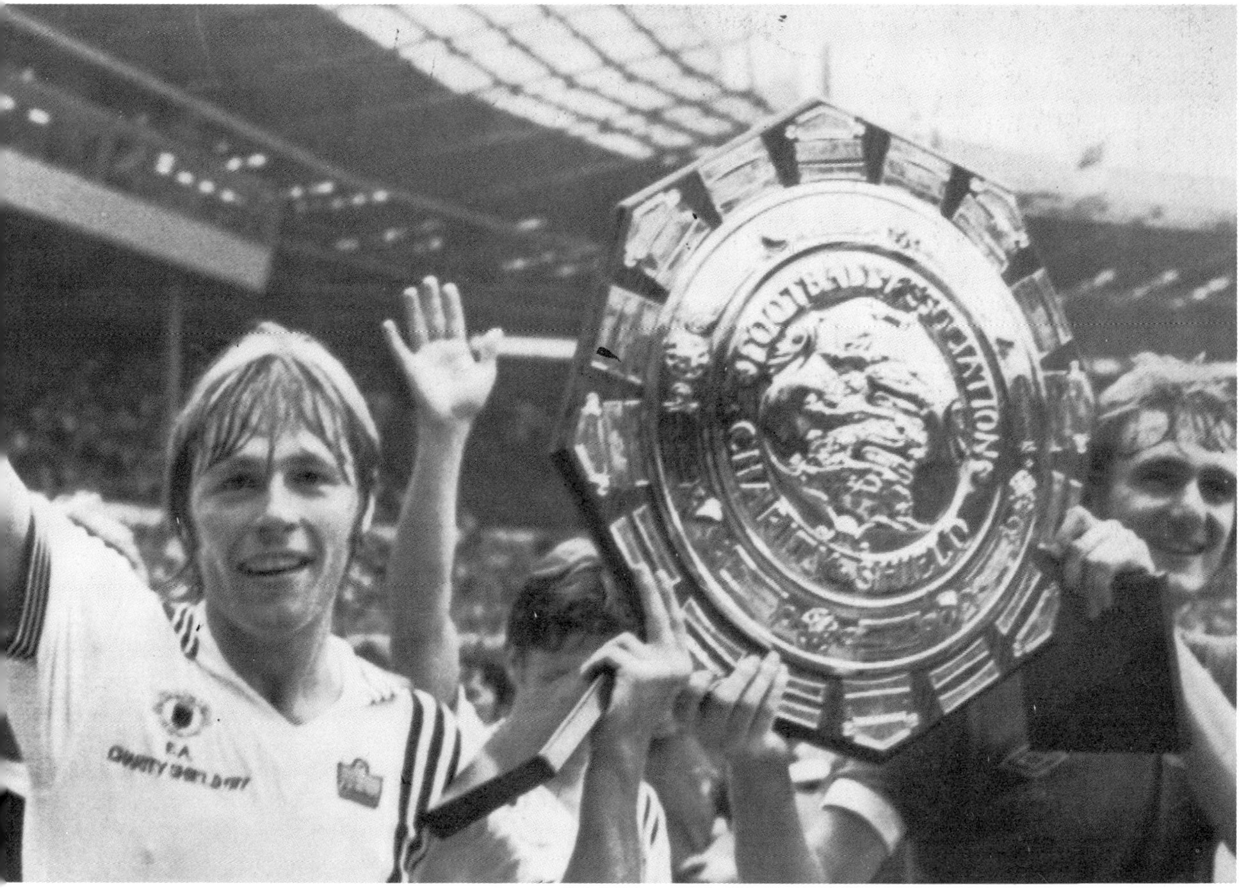

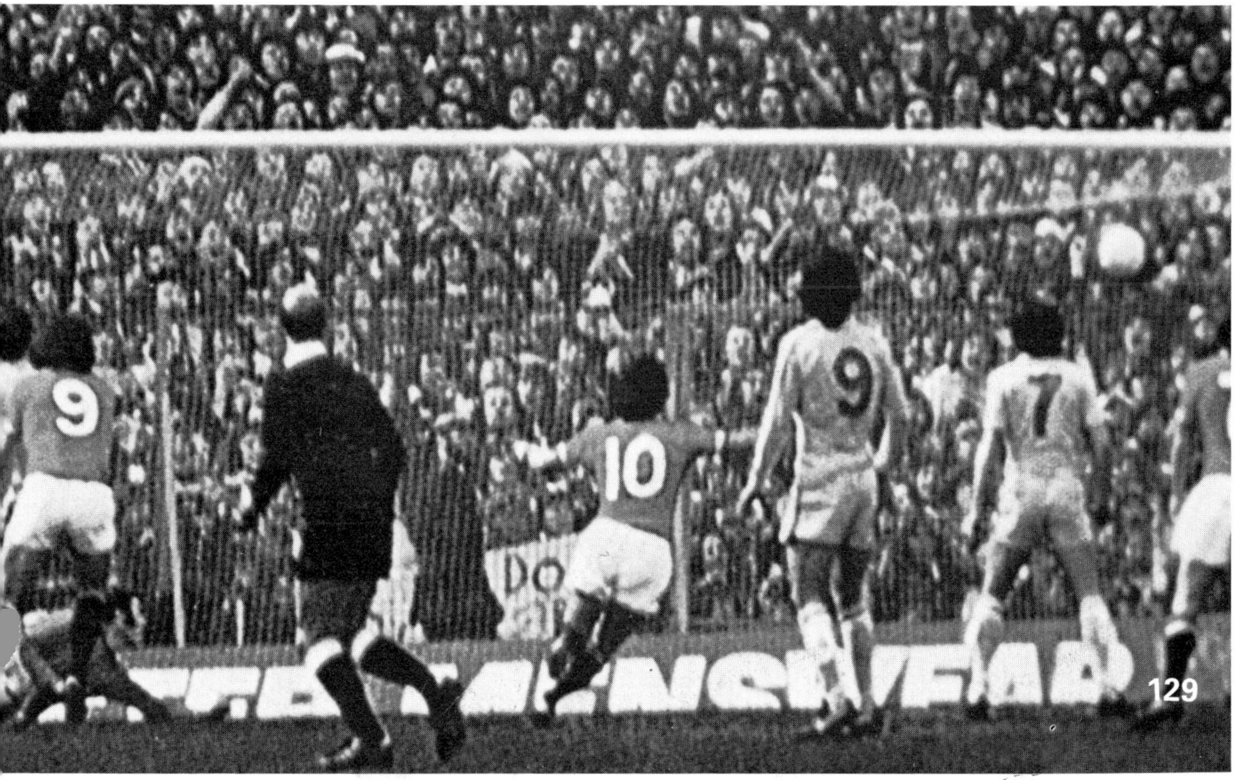

HERO OF
THE HOUR

IT'S a last-gasp equaliser for Liverpool against United in the 1979 F.A. Cup semi-final, and the scorer is Alan Hansen. But here (inset) is the man whose upraised arm signals triumph in the Goodison Park replay ... for Jimmy Greenhoff's goal took United on to Wembley.

HEARTACHE OF THE SEASON

IT WAS 2–0 at Wembley, and Arsenal were cruising to victory in the 1979 F.A. Cup final. Then Gordon McQueen struck, and the game was wide open again. When Sammy McIlroy struck this second goal past Pat Jennings (above), it was the signal for Mickey Thomas and Gordon McQueen, and their team-mates, to salute Sammy (left) ... but their joy turned to heartache as Arsenal rapped straight back with a goal which was the winner out of five.

131

SOCCER'S UPS AND DOWNS

FOOTBALL can be a funny game, and no-one knows this better than Matt Busby, who has sampled just about everything Soccer has to offer. So have Manchester United . . . triumph and tragedy have been interwoven with the club's history. These pictures show various sides of Soccer—United with the Charity Shield, and a rousing homecoming after defeat in the 1976 F.A. Cup final. And below, it's delight for United, despair for Derby as Joe Jordan congratulates marksman Sammy McIlroy, while 'keeper David McKellar and defenders Keith Osgood (No. 6), Steve Buckley (No. 3) and David Langan (on the ground) see things from a different viewpoint. The spring of 1980 saw Derby going down . . . just as United had done a few years previously.

MANCHESTER

versus

MATT BUSBY'S United take on his former club, Liverpool, in a battle between Manchester and Merseyside. Above, a League game at Anfield, with Phil Neal beating Gary Bailey. Right, another Anfield occasion, featuring Steve Heighway and Steve Coppell.
BELOW, the 1977 F.A. Cup final, with Jimmy Nicholl and Jimmy Case in a ballet-type duel. Bottom right, another League tussle, with Gordon McQueen blocking a shot from Kenny Dalglish.

MERSEYSIDE

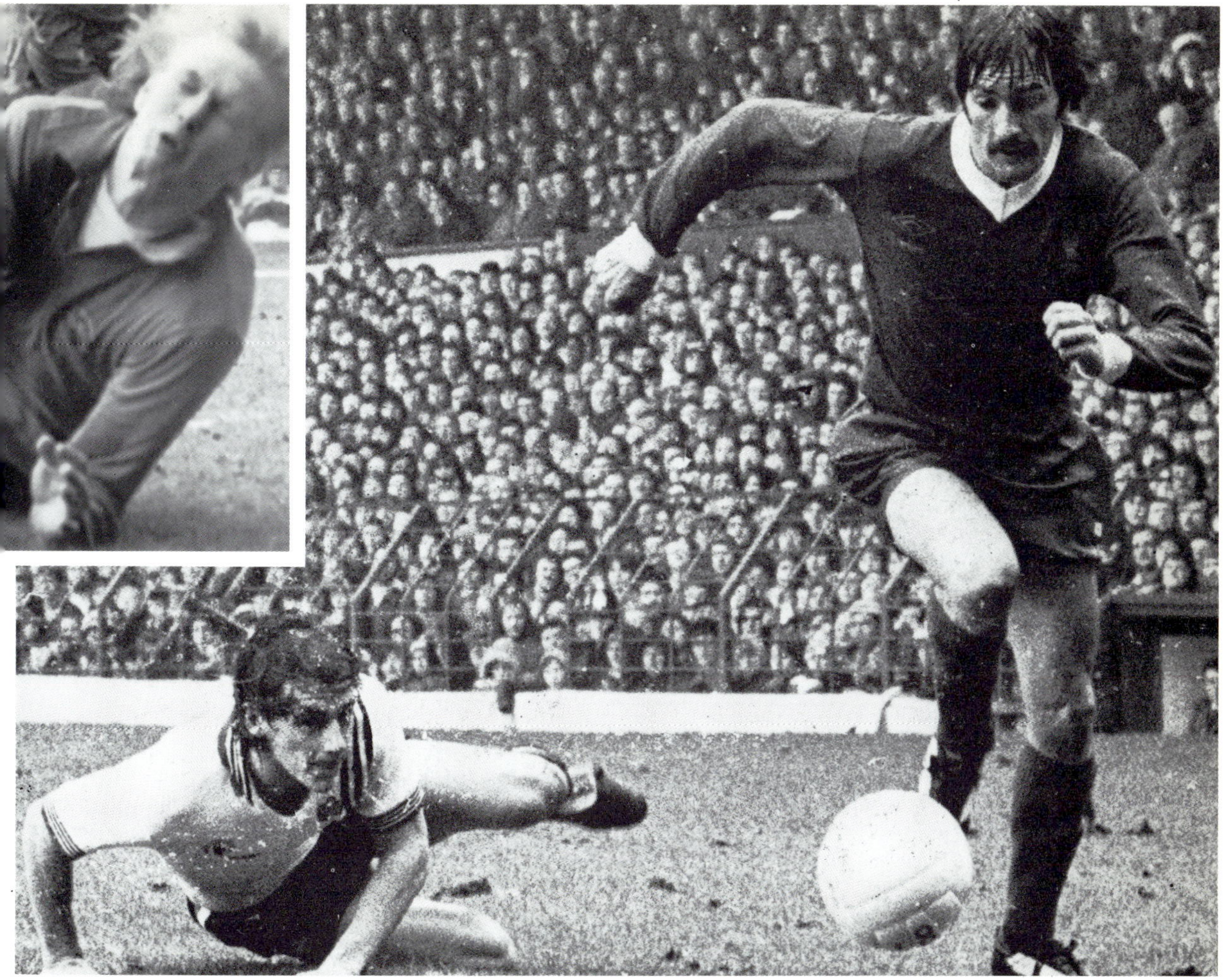

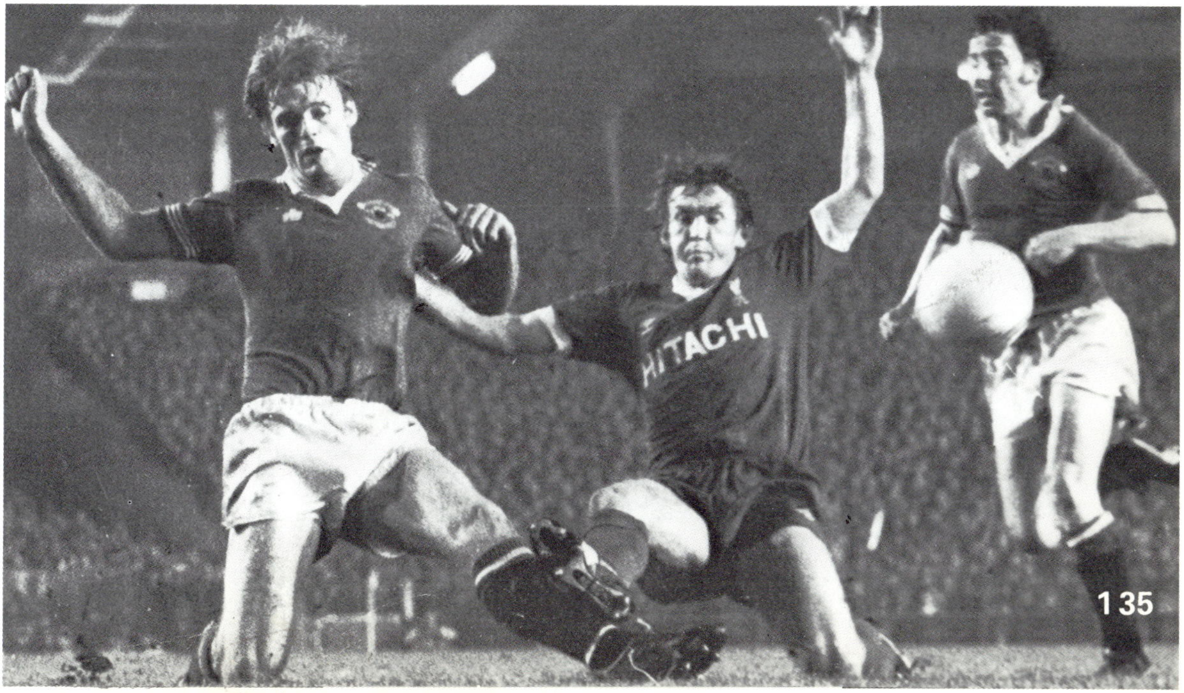
HITACHI

RIVALS ON THE FIELD OF PLAY—BUT THE BEST OF FRIENDS OFF IT

WEMBLEY ACTION featuring Manchester United and Liverpool (top picture) in the 1977 F.A. Cup final, and this Jimmy Case shot counted as an equaliser for Liverpool, though United had the last laugh, as they claimed the trophy with a 2–1 victory. But when the action has ceased, rivals can resume their friendship, as the picture above illustrates. It's an Anfield get-together of United and Liverpool directors, with Sir Matt Busby and Liverpool chairman Mr. John W. Smith linking arms, as the camera catches the sporting spirit of two of Soccer's most illustrious clubs.

AS WELL as being president of Manchester United, Sir Matt Busby is a member of the Football League management committee and of the Football Association's international committee. And here is a get-together of the latter committee, with directors from various clubs taking time off to pose for the cameraman. Back row (left to right): Messrs. A. Odell, B. Millichip, L. Webb, J. Wiseman, R. Speake, E. Croker, E. Kangley, L. Smart and N. Hillier. Front row: Messrs. J. Thomas, P. J. Swales and R. Wragg, Professor Sir Harold Thompson, and Sir Matt Busby.

MANAGERS WHO HAVE FOLLOWED IN MY FOOTSTEPS

FOUR men have followed Matt Busby as manager of Manchester United. Top left, Wilf McGuinness, one-time United player; top right, Frank O'Farrell; bottom left, Tommy Docherty; bottom right, Dave Sexton, currently on a new, three-year contract.

AND ONE WHO DECLINED, WITH THANKS

ABOVE, the man who declined, with thanks . . . Jock Stein, of Celtic and Scotland fame.

DIRECTORS, as well as managers, come under fire at times, and I am experienced enough to know that there has been speculation as to how much power I have wielded since I occupied a seat in the boardroom at Old Trafford.

To put it bluntly: can I be criticised because—as the speculation has been—I have not let managers get on with their jobs?

The answer: when I considered it right, I have expressed my opinion . . . but I have never interfered with the manager's right to do the job the way he thinks best. I wouldn't have thanked directors for getting on my back when I was a manager, and I

don't believe any of the various people who succeeded me as team boss at Manchester United can claim that I over-rode them.

As a manager, it was never my policy to tell lies, although it was my job to keep the club's business secret, as the occasion demanded; particularly in the matter of transfers. However, I tried never to duck issues, even when parrying pointed questions.

Now, as a director, I have seen life from the other side of the Soccer fence, and I am not naive enough to think that people won't have some pointed questions about my sphere of influence at Manchester United in my present capacity. I shall be as honest now as I tried to be when I occupied the managerial chair. So

I HAVE NEVER INTERFERED WITH THE MANAGER'S RIGHT TO DO THE JOB

RIGHT, Tommy Cavanagh, right-hand man to both Tommy Docherty and Dave Sexton; far right, Alex Stepney—he made a comeback after having been dropped by Tommy Docherty; top right, with Matt Busby, Denis Law and Bobby Charlton. Wilf McGuinness took the decision to drop these players, and (says Matt Busby) 'his decision was respected, even if it caused some raised eyebrows.'

first, let me give you the background to my decision to quit.

In 1966, after Partizan Belgrade had knocked us out of the European Cup, I was at my lowest ebb since the Munich air crash, and it was in my mind to turn my back on football altogether. It seemed the fates had conspired against the club and myself, and I remember telling Paddy Crerand: 'We'll never win the European Cup now.'

In fact, we had to wait until 1968, and in the meantime, I had to be content with Paddy's assurance, 'We will win it for you, boss', although his timing was a little bit out.

I have described already seeing the blind children crossing the road, and suddenly realising that I was in danger of getting my priorities wrong. I also came under pressure from my wife, Jean, who kept hammering into me that the people killed at Munich would have wanted me to see the job through. So I did.

Even so, as time went by after the European Cup triumph of 1968, I felt increasingly that the years were catching up with me, that I was feeling the pressures of the job more than I liked. At one stage, I considered going away for a couple of months to think about things, for I felt I had had enough.

So when, eventually, I took the decision to quit, it had not been made on the spur of the moment. And

when I told the board how I felt, I had to withstand some strenuous efforts to dissuade me.

When the directors saw that I was not to be moved, they accepted the inevitable with good grace, and generously made provision for me to join them on the board. At which point it became obvious that Manchester United must find a new manager.

Let me say here and now that I was largely responsible for the appointments of Wilf McGuinness, Frank O'Farrell, Tommy Docherty and Dave Sexton in turn . . . but never at any time did I interfere in their management of the team.

I always supported them, even if I felt that they were wrong—and whether it turned out that I was right or not. Unfortunately, some things didn't work out right for the men or the club.

It is an open secret that during the time Wilf McGuinness was manager—and it had been at my suggestion that he was given his head—loyalties among players became divided and, as a result, the atmosphere in the dressing-room was not all that it might have been. In the final analysis, it seemed that some senior players were not happy about Wilf's handling of affairs.

Wilf might well have decided the time had come to assert his own authority; but, inevitably, matters reached a stage where the subject of the management came up at boardroom level. Wilf must be given

RIGHT, Paddy Roche in action, and smiling through, despite a nightmare experience when he was pitched into United's first team.

ABOVE (left), winger Gordon Hill, who was signed by Tommy Docherty for United, then followed him on to Derby County and Queen's Park Rangers.

credit for having taken United to two Cup semi-finals, but at the end it was agreed by the board that action must be taken.

I was sad to see him go, though I concurred with the general boardroom verdict and, reluctantly, I took charge again. Although we had a reasonable run, when I was asked by some of the players to carry on, I told them: 'I've really had enough.' So United began again to look for a new manager.

Jock Stein became the target, and Glasgow Celtic allowed us to approach him. But finally, Jock declined with thanks.

Our thoughts turned to Leicester City and Frank O'Farrell, who had steered them to promotion. United's late chairman, Louis Edwards was given permission by Leicester's Len Shipman to approach Frank, and I met him at his home. The sequel was that Frank became manager of Manchester United.

After a spell when it seemed United might just win the First Division championship, the going got rougher and results worsened; and eventually, the question of the management arose again. I did suggest giving Frank a short while longer, but the over-riding view was to the contrary, and I didn't rock the boat.

Tommy Docherty arrived at Old Trafford after he had indicated his interest in the job—as it happened, when I met him at a match—and everyone knows

how United went down, regained First Division status and won the F.A. Cup. Everyone knows, also, the sequel. So Tommy Docherty left Old Trafford.

Dave Sexton became manager at the second time of asking, in effect, for after he had taken Chelsea to the F.A. Cup final in 1970, Manchester United took discreet soundings as to his situation at Stamford Bridge. The information that came our way was that Dave believed he should stay loyal to a team which had done well for him, and we respected such loyalty.

After Tommy Docherty's departure from Old Trafford, I advised the board to try for Dave, who by then was at Queen's Park Rangers. They agreed to release him, and this time he did not hesitate to take on the United job.

Perhaps it will serve to confirm my earlier statement that I have never interfered with team management if I give one or two examples.

For instance, there was an occasion when Wilf McGuinness decided to drop Bobby Charlton and Denis Law. His decision was respected, even if it caused some raised eyebrows.

You may recall Tommy Docherty giving Denis Law a free transfer and, at a later time, dropping Alex

139

IN action for United against Liverpool . . . Brian Greenhoff. Matt Busby says: 'I wasn't happy about him being allowed to leave United for Leeds, but the decision was up to the manager. The manager must be allowed the freedom to do his job, back his judgment, stand on his own feet.'

Stepney and promoting Paddy Roche. I didn't fully agree with either decision, but I didn't block the manager's moves.

The first I really heard about the Law business was at a board meeting when Tommy Docherty revealed his plans for the future. They didn't include Denis Law. I made the point—and I felt it was valid—that Denis should be retained, even if he played in only 50

per cent of the matches, because he was still likely to contribute some valuable goals.

Tommy Docherty felt otherwise. He was the manager, was prepared to back his judgment . . . so what he said went, even if I wasn't at all happy about his decision.

When the news broke, it seemed that Denis had learned via the media that he was being turfed out on a free transfer. It certainly made headline news. I wasn't happy about the way the matter became public, for in all my managerial dealings I had made a point of telling the player before anyone else.

It may all have been due to a misunderstanding; it may never have been the intention that the news should become public before Law himself had been told. But once it had happened, it was unfortunate, to say the least. Nevertheless, that was that.

When Paddy Roche was promoted to the first team, I felt that he was a goalkeeper with genuine potential—but to suggest, as Tommy Docherty did, that he was there to stay was ludicrous, because no manager can budget for future events so dogmatically.

I thought that in saying Roche was the man for the future, the manager had put the lad under extra pressure, and, for what it was worth, I was sure that Stepney—who made it clear *he* disagreed with Tommy Docherty—would be back after a few games. As, indeed, he was.

It was not because I had no faith in the manager's judgment, not because I lacked faith in Roche, either; but I knew my Alex Stepney, and when he said he would back his record against The Doc's judgment, I felt Stepney would be determined to regain his place by his own displays in the reserves.

Eventually, Tommy Docherty had to admit that he had been wrong—and he deserves credit for being big enough to say so publicly, too.

As United's manager, he did a tremendous amount of wheeling and dealing in the transfer market, and I can say categorically that whether I agreed or disagreed with his signings and his sales, I gave my wholehearted support, once a decision had been taken. I have never stopped a signing going through, never halted a transfer deal out from Old Trafford.

My view was—and still is—that the manager must be allowed the freedom to do his job, to back his judgment, to stand on his own feet.

There have been three outstanding examples of this stand during the reign of Dave Sexton. I wasn't happy about Brian Greenhoff being allowed to leave Manchester United for Leeds, but the decision was up to the manager. I had reservations about letting Andy Ritchie go, but Dave put up a good case for letting the player have the last word. When an offer of close on £400,000 was made, Dave felt he had to be fair to Ritchie in telling him about it and letting him decide what he wanted to do. So the decision was left that

ANDY RITCHIE, *the striker who could have moved on for close on £400,000. Matt Busby says: 'I had reservations about letting him go, but Dave Sexton put up a good case for letting the player have the last word. Ritchie said he wanted to stay.'*

way, and Ritchie said he wanted to stay.

In the case of Ray Wilkins, we knew that Dave had been keen to sign him for months, and he was given the go-ahead to negotiate, although the board—and this was their right—decided just how far to go when it came to a fee. Chelsea wanted more than we were prepared to pay. Dave wanted Ray Wilkins. Eventually, the directors backed him all the way and paid the price.

I believe these instances show that since I stepped down from the managerial chair, I have not tried to run Manchester United as a Matt Busby show. Rather I have tried to do my best, as always, for the club. And let me say I believe there have been times when United, because of their unique position in British football, have been held to ransom in the transfer market when clubs have thought we should pay a price that lesser rivals couldn't.

MANAGER Dave Sexton (above) had been keen to sign Ray Wilkins (left) for months. Matt Busby says: 'Chelsea wanted more than we were prepared to pay . . . Dave wanted Ray . . . eventually, the directors backed him all the way and paid the price.'

It would be remiss of me if I didn't say a word or two about the United supporters who, in my view, have helped to make the club an institution. We know there are some so-called fans who have embarrassed us and caused trouble which has besmirched the good name of Manchester United. But, in the main, we can only be thankful to the thousands who have proved they are loyal supporters, through good times and bad.

I think it can be summed up by saying that when United have a home gate of maybe 45,000, it becomes a subject for comment . . . because it's unusually low. How many clubs would dearly love to command an attendance such as that every *other* home game?

Our supporters have shown themselves to be utterly dedicated to United and, in all modesty, I believe I can claim my efforts through the years have had a fair amount to do with the support the club generates. More than that: it gives me pleasure to say so, because, generally speaking, I think that people accept that I have played my part in the making of a truly great club. So I see no reason to apologise for the contribution I have made. Indeed, I took pride in the fact that I became the first president of Manchester United. I also deemed it a great honour when, at the annual awards dinner of the Professional Footballers' Association in the spring of 1980, I received a special Merit Award in recognition of the contribution I had made to football.

I mentioned managers a short while back, and I will go on record as saying that I have been very happy with the way Dave Sexton has conducted the affairs of Manchester United. At one stage, the fans gave him a rough ride; I didn't feel they were giving him enough time.

It's true to day that you won't pick up the paper and find Dave making flamboyant statements which make you feel embarrassed. Equally, perhaps, he doesn't display himself sufficiently. He pales in comparison with Tommy Docherty, for instance, because The Doc was always good for a quote during his time as United's team boss.

I have a great deal of time for Dave Sexton, in every respect, and at the start of the 1980s I felt that, after a hesitant beginning, not only was he becoming accepted by the United fans, but his solid ground-work was showing signs of something really good. It was beginning to look like the Manchester United of old. After going to Wembley in 1979, United made a brave bid for the title the following season.

On a personal note, I was surprised that the news about my connection with the Red Devils Souvenir Shop at Old Trafford made headlines—because I had been firmly under the impression that people generally knew I owned the shop. But to remove any doubts, let me tell the story of how it developed.

A year before I retired as manager, I had an idea about taking over the souvenir shop which, at that time, was doing only fair business. When I did retire, I told the board I would be prepared to pay for the stock and take the shop over, and it was as simple as that. In a way, I became one of the pioneers of the souvenir-shop industry.

Let us be clear about one thing. There was no secrecy about my move; neither did I feel I should have to advertise it to the world. Furthermore, my business venture could just as easily have blown up in my face, rather than turn out to be a success. So I took a gamble, off my own bat.

When the subject was raised at the club's annual general meeting, reference was made to the fact that the souvenir shop didn't figure in the club's accounts. It couldn't, because the shop is owned privately, by myself. And my family has an interest in it.

I immediately made this clear to the shareholders, and my answer was accepted happily enough.

Finally, football and knighthoods. And again, I don't have to apologise to anyone for accepting my own knighthood. I had not the slightest doubt, from the first moment that I was asked if I would be prepared to become known as Sir Matt Busby, about accepting. I saw it as a great honour, in recognition of what I had done for Manchester United and, to a degree, for football in general.

It brought one problem. After my visit to Buckingham Palace, people began to tell me they weren't quite sure how to address me. I soon put matters in perspective: if they had known me as 'Matt' before, I was still 'Matt' to them; though I didn't expect to be addressed familiarly as 'Matt' by perfect strangers. Once a relationship has been established, the formalities can be dropped, although there is clearly a place and a time for the 'Sir Matt Busby' to be used.

But throughout my life, I don't believe I have ever been accused of snobbery, and I have tried to be helpful and friendly whenever possible. Sir Matt Busby I may be today . . . but I'm still the same man at heart as I was when I arrived in Manchester all those years ago.

MOMENTS TO REMEMBER

RIGHT, Matt Busby, C.B.E., with Sword of Honour for services to the game, and attired in top hat as he leaves Buckingham Palace after having been knighted.

BELOW, farewell as manager of Manchester United in 1969, and the 1979 homecoming from the F.A. Cup final.